THE

MENTALLY ILL

MENTOR

**PRACTICAL PRINCIPLES FOR ACHIEVING
AND MAINTAINING BALANCE IN YOUR LIFE**

- AN INSPIRING TRUE STORY -
DAVID GRANT MILLER

Disclaimer: The information contained in The Mentally Ill Mentor is not
intended to be a substitute for professional medical advice. The author does
not give medical advice or prescribe the use of any technique as a form of
treatment for Mental Illness. In the event that you use any of the information contained in this book for yourself, the author and publisher assume no
responsibility for your actions.

Note: For reasons of privacy, names and some details have been changed.

Website: www.TheMentallyIllMentor.com

Note for Librarians: A cataloguing record for this book is available from Library
and Archives Canada at www.collectionscanada.ca/amicus/index-e.html

ISBN 1-4120-6051-6

Printed in Victoria, BC, Canada. Printed on paper with minimum 30%
recycled fibre. Trafford's print shop runs on "green energy" from solar, wind
and other environmentally-friendly power sources.

TRAFFORD
PUBLISHING™

Offices in Canada, USA, Ireland and UK
This book was published on-demand in cooperation with Trafford Publishing.
On-demand publishing is a unique process and service of making a book
available for retail sale to the public taking advantage of on-demand
manufacturing and Internet marketing. On-demand publishing includes
promotions, retail sales, manufacturing, order fulfilment, accounting and
collecting royalties on behalf of the author.

Book sales for North America and international:
Trafford Publishing, 6E–2333 Government St.,
Victoria, BC v8t 4p4 CANADA
phone 250 383 6864 (toll-free 1 888 232 4444)
fax 250 383 6804; email to orders@trafford.com
Book sales in Europe:
Trafford Publishing (uk) Ltd., Enterprise House, Wistaston Road Business
Centre,
Wistaston Road, Crewe, Cheshire cw2 7rp UNITED KINGDOM
phone 01270 251 396 (local rate 0845 230 9601)
facsimile 01270 254 983; orders.uk@trafford.com
Order online at: trafford.com/05-0952

10 9 8 7 6 5 4

DEDICATION

To Aimee, my eternal companion and best friend:
You are the love of my life.

To Thomas, Harrison, Julianna and Jacob:
You are the sunshine in my life.

THANK YOU

Thank you Aimee, for your encouragement, support,
and unending faith in me.

Thank you to my children for sacrificing time with Dad
so I could finish my book.

Thank you to my parents, my parents-in-law, and numerous
other people who have contributed in so many ways to making
this dream a reality.

CONTENTS

Introduction

SO, WHAT *EXACTLY* IS A MENTOR?

The dictionary defines a Mentor as: *A wise and trusted counselor or teacher.*

If wisdom comes from experience, I guess you could say I have a lot of it. But the kind of experience I have is much different than nearly all of the people that currently advise you on what to do about your struggle with a Mental Illness.

You see, unlike nearly all of *them*, *I* have actually been there. I have *actually felt* the shame and lived through the sorrow. I have *actually shed the tears* and felt the desperation. I have *actually* kept on going when everything inside me said it was time to just give up.

As much as your doctor, your therapist, your social worker, your spouse, your brother or sister, your mother or father, your best friend or whomever it is, may love and care about you - *they just don't know how you feel.*

I do.

MY TRUE STORY

Fresh out of a "real-for-real" Mental Institution after a bizarre trip to Nevada in search of *The* Jessica Simpson, I was *sure* my life was over. Not only had I been officially diagnosed with a "debilitating" Mental Illness, but I had no job, no money, no self-esteem and no desire to go on living.

As the painful days following my hospitalizations turned into weeks and then months, I struggled *just to get out of bed* each day. I hated myself for that, and for the fact I was neglecting my responsibilities as a husband, a father, and a provider. I also hated the fact that my future seemed even more hopeless and dark than the present.

Back then, during every waking moment, hard, cruel questions would swirl around in my confused mind - questions like: How am I ever going to provide for my wife and our three young children? How long can I endure barely being able to pay the rent and put food on the table? What if I let my Mental Illness get out of control again? How long will my wife, Aimee, be able to put up with me before she resorts to divorce?

NOW OR NEVER

Unable to answer these questions, I finally came up with the *perfect* solution.

Although I had tried to put the almost constant thought out of my mind for months, I finally decided that taking my own life would be the most appropriate way to deal with the overwhelming shame and hopelessness I felt. After all, how could someone *officially* diagnosed with a Mental Illness and who had spent time in mental institutions in two different countries on three separate occasions, ever make it in the world?

I still remember clearly the day when I realized it was now or never.

My wife, our two young children and our new baby were at a birthday party. I knew I could leave an "explanation letter" on the front door, which only *she* would be able to read. The children would never see my dead body, and in the long run they wouldn't even remember me. Not only would my wife be relieved of me – the biggest burden of her entire life – she would finally be provided for financially by a life insurance policy I knew included suicide.

But as I pictured it in my mind's eye – actually walking downstairs, loading my gun, putting it to my head and pulling the trigger – *something* or *someone* stopped me. From deep within my soul I felt a faint ray of hope, a feeling that I *was* worth something and that my life *was* worth living.

A CRY FOR HELP

Instead of being worried that I would be bothering my wife, or that her friends at the birthday party would think I was some kind of crazy, unemployed nut, I called her up and begged her to come home. When she finally arrived, I cried like a baby as I poured out the feelings of my heart to her.

It was in that moment I realized for the first time that major, immediate, sweeping life change was no longer a matter of preference for me. *It had become a matter of life and death.*

As much as I wanted to continue to blame my childhood, my marriage, my failed businesses and all the people around me for the bottomless emotional pit that held me captive, doing so would only be *continuing* the lie I had unknowingly been telling myself for years. It would be feeding the *very* thing that had brought me to this point in my life. It would perpetuate the deadly cycle that I was just beginning to realize I was in.

The fact was, I had finally hit absolute rock bottom. And although I was in excruciating emotional pain, I was still around to talk about it. Somehow, through a literal miracle, I had resisted my terrible temptation. And from that point on, I realized that I had nowhere to go but up. While I was full of fear and anxiety, I also knew that somehow, someday – against all odds – I would finally reach the top, crawl out, and declare victory.

• • •

THE TRUTH

In that moment I made a firm resolve. I promised myself I would never give up on *me* – and living my life – ever again, no matter how hopeless it seemed. From that day forward, although I still struggled with feelings of depression for awhile, my *attitude* did a complete 180.

Since committing suicide was no longer an option, I decided I might as well face my problems. But to *effectively* deal with them, I knew I would need to somehow figure out how to *overcome* my Mental Illness. With that in mind, instead of continuing to wallow in my misery, I got my attitude in gear and got busy.

GETTING OUT OF BED

First on my list of problems to solve was motivating myself to get out of bed by 8 in the morning, instead of noon or 2 o'clock. While I still felt too unsure of myself to look for work, I knew that if I could just consistently get out of bed at a decent hour each morning my sense of accomplishment would eventually convert itself into the self-esteem I lacked.

After some deep thought, and with a little bit of fear, I picked up the phone and made a life-changing call, one I had been procrastinating for months. After explaining that I *didn't* commit a crime and that I didn't *need* community service hours, I made an appointment with the local Food Bank. The next morning I reported at 8am sharp (well, almost), and realized that I was needed. For the first time in months I forgot about *me* and *my* problems and became focused on helping others. With a new sense of purpose, I continued to volunteer at the Food Bank, finding it easier and easier to get out of bed each morning.

MY RESEARCH

After willingly putting in my two hours at the Food Bank, instead of going home and risking getting sucked back into bed for another 4 hours, I would head directly to the library of the local community college. In this quiet, serene atmosphere I would lose myself in a new-found passion – reading.

Not wanting to waste what little time I would have without a job, I immersed myself in all the "self-help" literature I could get my hands on. I ate up books like *The 7 Habits of Highly Effective People* by Stephan Covey, *Stand Up for Your Life*, by Cheryl Richardson, *Awaken the Giant Within,* by Tony Robbins, *The Power of Positive Thinking* by Norman Vincent Peale, *You Can Heal Your Life* by Louise Hay and *Life Strategies*, by Dr. Phil. I also became intrigued with the true success stories of people like Mary Kay Ash, Nelson Mandela, Mother Theresa, Abraham Lincoln, Og Mandino and many, many others.

In that college library, hours passed like minutes as I became lost in another world – a world full of the great thoughts, great ideas and success stories of great people. As I continued to read, day after day after day, I thought deeply about all the ways I could apply my learning in my quest to overcome my Mental Illness.

MY LIGHT BULB EXPERIENCE

After a few months, I decided to target my "research" and focus specifically on books about Mental Illness. Not surprisingly, my search on the subject of "Mental Illness" brought up a long list of books. But as

I slowly began reading each summary listed on the computer screen it seemed that none of them had the type of information I was looking for.

Believing the summaries just weren't doing the books justice, I quickly scrawled down five that appeared interesting and went to the shelf. Unfortunately, however, I soon discovered that the summaries were bang on. Although the books *appeared* "credible" (they were written by experienced medical professionals or relatives of someone who had struggled with a Mental Illness) every single one failed to meet my expectations. Instead of an easy-to-follow, step-by-step guide to overcoming a Mental Illness, I found either boring technical explanations or scary, disheartening stories.

Determined to find something better, I continued my search for hours as book after book after book seemed to focus on how rough my sorry life would be now that I had been diagnosed with a real-for-real Mental Illness.

Not wanting to stop until I at least found *some* of the information I was looking for, I finally read a line that convinced me that the time for reading books on Mental Illness was over! That simple sentence was a sister's sorrowful description of what I *thought* was the *suicide* of her brother. But reading just a little further, and to my amazement, I discovered that when she described "*losing*" her brother to schizophrenia, she wasn't referring to his tragic death, but his now - tragic life! In not so many words, the unspoken but clear message was: Now that he has a Mental Illness, *he might as well be dead*!!!

Shaking my head in disbelief, I put the book down and decided I had had enough.

DALE CARNEGIE'S STORY

Shortly after, I decided it was high time for *me* to do exactly what Dale Carnegie did.

Desperately wanting to overcome his tendency to worry, he searched a university library for books that would teach him how. But when he found *nine times* the number of books on "worms" than "worry", he decided it was time to write his own. The end product, *How to Stop Worrying and Start Living* became a bestseller.

IS *MY* BOOK FOR *YOU*?

If you or a loved one is struggling with a Mental Illness, this book is *definitely* for you. You see, it's kinda the "Reader's Digest Condensed Version" of the hundreds of *useful* self-help books I've studied over the past four years. Mixed with personal insights and true life experiences, *The Mentally Ill Mentor* will show you that being diagnosed with a Mental Illness *can* turn into the best thing that ever happened to you.

UM...I DON'T THINK SO!

In a nutshell, this book will show you how you or a loved one can eventually overcome a Mental Illness and achieve a state of Life – Long Mental Wellness & Success. The great thing is, once you realize and accept that you have a real-for-real mental problem, you are already half way to overcoming it.

So, how is *my* book any different than all the others on the shelf? Here are just two differences:

1. *The Mentally Ill Mentor* will take you "inside" the mind of someone who has actually struggled with a Mental Illness – *me*.

2. This book will teach you important principles and provide a simple step-by-step program for overcoming a Mental Illness and creating for yourself Life – Long Mental Wellness & Success.

So how do I know that what I'm saying is true? Bottom Line: Every principle, every technique, every strategy, every tip in this book is a part of who I now am. In short, my current state of Mental Wellness & Success has come about as a direct result of trying my very best to practice what I preach.

OK, SO WHAT WILL I LEARN?

Things you will *not* learn in this book are techniques such as: how to ditch your doctor, avoid seeing your psychiatrist, or escape being institutionalized. In fact, after reading *The Mentally Ill Mentor,* you may decide that professional medical advice and assistance is *exactly* what you need.

What you will learn, however, is how to begin adopting new beliefs about yourself and your Mental Illness. You will learn fundamental principles and specific techniques which, when internalized and followed consistently over time, will empower you to overcome your Mental Illness and live a normal, happy, productive, successful life.

WHAT THIS BOOK CAN DO FOR YOU

In the same way that just *thinking* about exercise won't make you skinny, the principles and techniques taught in *The Mentally Ill Mentor* will only be effective if you (or your loved one) hops on the treadmill and starts working up a sweat. And, while I really, really hope you decide to put in the effort, that life - altering decision is all yours.

WHAT DOES "OVERCOMING" A MENTAL ILLNESS LOOK LIKE?

"Overcoming" Mental Illness looks kinda like this:

- You willingly accept full responsibility for your Mental Illness.
- You love yourself and accept yourself unconditionally.
- You consistently apply basic self-maintenance principles which form the base of your mental stability.
- You monitor and analyze your progress and make adjustments as necessary.
- When you encounter challenges you are prepared, and deal with them in a mature, emotionally balanced way.
- You find satisfaction in continuing to improve yourself little by little, day by day.

FROM "OVERCOMING" TO "LIFE - LONG MENTAL WELLNESS & SUCCESS"

Over the course of days, months, years or even decades of *consistently* applying these fundamental principles, you will graduate from a state of "overcoming" your Mental Illness to a state of Mental Wellness and Success.

When the implementation of these principles and techniques becomes so much a part of who you are that you follow them almost without thinking, you will know you have arrived.

In contrast to "overcoming" a Mental Illness, creating and maintaining Life – Long Mental Wellness looks more like this:

- The fear or "threat" of a Mental Illness is no longer an issue for you.

- Self-love and unconditional self-acceptance is part of who you are.

- You are comfortable and confident with the way you are living your life.

- Setting and achieving your goals is a habit.

- Relationships with the most important people in your life are great and improving every day.

- You are, unquestionably, in control of your life, your dreams, and your destiny.

- You love yourself, the person you have become, and the even better person you are striving to be.

- You thoroughly enjoy life and are up to the task when it comes to overcoming challenges.

- You have become accustomed to each day being filled with a quiet inner peace and happiness.

9/11

When terrorists blew up the World Trade Centers, America and the world was changed forever. That terrible day everyone's focus was on the horror of this senseless tragedy. But since that time, heartwarming stories of sacrifice and hope have also come to light.

Emergency workers risked their lives, and in many cases died, in an effort to save their fellow citizens. The residents of several small towns in Eastern Canada opened their homes to thousands of Americans stranded when all air traffic in North America was grounded. Across the continent strangers came together in an effort to help each other.

THE TSUNAMI

On December 26, 2004, this phenomenon of people helping people was played out again when an earthquake below the Indian Ocean created a massive wave killing hundreds of thousands of people in South Asia. In response to this horrific tragedy, an unprecedented number of donations were given. People, corporations and governments opened their hearts *and* their wallets to help brothers and sisters *they didn't even know.*

BECOMING A MENTOR

While the results of an out-of-control Mental Illness can be just as tragic as a terrorist attack or a destructive natural disaster, I take courage in believing that you and I, and the millions of people who struggle with Mental Illness can help each other out.

This will happen as we all work toward two main goals:

1. Becoming Well, and maintaining this state for the rest of our lives.

2. Becoming a Mentor, or role model for others who are still struggling to become Mentally Well.

As we are successful in achieving these two goals, I believe there will be two main positive outcomes:

1. We will create for ourselves a life of happiness that flows from a deep sense of inner peace.

2. We will find satisfaction, strength, and purpose in our lives.

As we continue working towards this common goal of taking care of our own Mental Wellness *first* and then helping others, I can see the day when the struggles and the pain associated with Mental Illness will become a thing of the past.

If you are willing to believe in this dream, keep reading. This book is *definitely* for you.

PART 1

MY TRUE STORY

WARNING!

If you or a loved one has ever struggled with a Mental Illness, there is a good chance you may find the following true story to be "emotionally charged". As one reader put it: "It made me laugh, it made me cry, it made me remember."

What you are about to read is not just a re-telling of what happened to me. Rather, Part 1, My True Story, is an account of the actual thoughts, feelings and experiences I had *during* my manic episode, and later, *during* my battle with depression.

CHAPTER 1

What Is Wrong With These People?!

" **S**cram, Dave! I wish I didn't have to do this to you, but you are no longer welcome in our house!"

And with that, I realized that my brother-in-law and his wife were just like my wife and the rest of the people who were supposed to love and take care of me in a time when I needed them most – a time when I was struggling. Really struggling. Here I was, hundreds of miles from home, assuming that my relatives would be the *first* ones I could count on in a time of need.

"Man, what a rip off," I thought to myself. "Here they are living in a big, beautiful mansion in Salt Lake City, on Timberline Drive of all places! They have lots of room to spare and now they want to kick me out!"

As hard as I tried to figure out what was wrong with them and why they seemed so annoyed with me all the time, I just couldn't put my finger on it. Maybe it was the fact that it was Christmas time and everyone was irritable from being up late too many nights in a row. Or maybe it was the financial stress of having to buy presents for everyone in a large extended family. But whatever it was, I was *really* getting sick of it. First my wife, then my brother-in-law, Derek, and now his wife, Anna?! What on earth was the problem with these people?!

As if that wasn't bad enough, another sister-in-law, Megan, was turning out to be two-faced. Also a guest in Derek and Anna's home, she had joined them in their efforts to be cruel to me and kick me out of the house! All this, when only two days before I had spent three hours on the phone pouring my heart out to her while I sat on the bed in my hotel room in Great Falls, Montana.

I called Megan just after getting home from the bar – something my strict morals and deeply held Christian values would not have normally allowed me to do. It was the first night after I left her sister, (my wife), Aimee, because of her never-ending attempts to control my life. I had explained to her that night on the phone that it was just more than I could bear. I just *had* to leave.

At the time I thought I could trust Megan! That night I had shared with her my most private thoughts about Aimee and my need to be free from her control, and how going to the bar gave me a sense of that freedom. And although I still felt it was important not to consume alcohol or break my vows of monogamy, I had told her how sometimes a guy just needs to be a guy – regardless of how long he has been married or how many children he has. In reality, I was just doing what I *should* have done years ago but resisted in the name of being responsible and doing the "right" thing. After all, I was only doing all the things normal 21-year-old guys do. I also told her that I felt this was a *special* situation. So special, in fact, that if my church leaders back home knew what I was up to, they would simply turn a blind eye. Throughout our conversation it had seemed as though she really cared about me. The fact was, however, she too had now turned against me.

But while I may have been down, I certainly was not out. I held my head high and replied confidently, "Derek, if you don't feel that you and

Anna are capable of helping me in a time of great need, I accept that. Something is obviously eating at you, and I agree that it *is* time for me to leave. Maybe I will come visit again when you are all feeling a little bit more like yourselves…I have really enjoyed our visits in the past. I'm sorry to have been such a burden on you this time."

And with that I walked into one of the many guest bedrooms, gathered up my clothes, and quickly and dutifully made my bed. Hesitating for only a moment, I left my note where it would easily be found the next time someone entered the room, and silently prayed that God would help Derek and Anna become nicer people.

After saying a quick goodbye, and being careful to avoid the normal hugs and "I love you's," I calmly walked out the back door, opened the gate, and said a disappointed "Goodbye, Colby," to the dog – the only one around who did not hate my guts.

CHAPTER 2

Resisting Satan's Temptation

As I put the key in the ignition and turned they key of my rusty 1986 Honda Accord, the engine "roared" to life – along with all the emotions I had been hiding. I wanted to make sure that the un-God-like treatment my relatives had chosen to show me – when I needed help the most – was *not* rewarded by them getting the best of me by making me cry or becoming upset. But as I pulled out of the driveway and began driving south on Timberline Drive, the weight of my sorrow hit me like a ton of bricks.

My tears flowed like a river as my soul cried out in sorrow. I felt much like a young infant abandoned by his mother. I felt so much despair, so much sadness, so much heartache, so much pain! All I could think was, "Why doesn't anyone love me anymore? Why, when I need them the most, would my relatives, and even my own wife, turn against me?! What on earth am I going to do?!"

Hundreds of miles from home with just a few hundred dollars in my pocket and only the clothes on my back, I felt completely alone. As my long, loud, cries of pain continued, my tears clouded my view as I sped up the windy, winter roads of Little Cottonwood Canyon.

Then, as if from God himself, I had the distinct impression that there was a *perfect* way to escape my pain. On one particularly sharp corner, featuring a very steep cliff, it was as if a voice inside my head, said,

"Listen up! Here is the answer to all your problems: Put the pedal to the metal, keep your wheel straight, and just keep driving."

Instantly, I realized that God would not tempt me to drive myself off a cliff. Instead, I knew it was Satan whispering in my ear and kicking me when I was down! "What a jerk!" I thought. Then, in a confident, no-nonsense, Dr. Phil - type voice, I said out loud: "If you think I am going to give into you, you've got another thing comin'." I will NOT commit suicide. I love myself and know that God is watching out for me. And not even you or your evil helpers are going to convince me to do something so utterly stupid!"

Having made myself clear, and wanting to further emphasize my point, I took my foot off the gas pedal and drove *under* the speed limit the rest of the way up the mountain. Slowly but surely, I was able to stop my tears as I thought about what to do next.

"Commit suicide?" I said out loud and shook my head. "As if!" Who did Satan think I was, some kind of weak - minded bone head? Did he really believe I would give into his temptation when I had the power of God backing me? Whatever the case, I decided that the smartest thing to do would be to put Satan out of my mind and focus on what God wanted for me. Then, recalling the "note" I had left in the bedroom at Derek and Anna's house, I devised a plan. If the plan worked, and if I sounded desperate enough, I was confident I could convince *someone* to give me the love and attention I needed.

Driving past the house again, I knew that there were many extended family members who had just arrived to celebrate New Year's Eve. While I didn't want to do anything too drastic, I reasoned that if I could just scare them a bit, maybe Derek and Anna would see it as a cry for help and welcome me back into their home.

I quickly drove north to the other end of Timberline Drive, turned right at the intersection, changed lanes, and then took a quick left into a gas station. Not more than six blocks from Derek and Anna's house, I deposited my coins into the payphone and made one of the most exciting phone calls of my life!

Unfortunately, Anna, the "control freak", answered the phone. In a disappointed but concerned tone of voice she casually asked where I was. I *told* her that I driven 25 miles South on I-95 and was calling from a payphone. I also casually mentioned the note I had left in my room and explained that it would be very important for her and everyone else in the house to read it. Then, at a moment of great suspense after Anna had asked, "What on earth is going on?!" I politely replied, "You'll see," and hung up the phone.

"Man, this is going to be fun!" I thought. Maybe the excitement will help everyone lighten up and see that I am not such a bad guy after all. It will be kinda like Mission Impossible – except this time it won't just be about money – it will be about them saving my life.

CHAPTER 3

Mission Impossible

My suicide note was actually a series of phrases scribbled on the back of over 20 business cards from the job I was sure I had lost by now.

Wanting to really suck them into believing I would *actually* commit suicide, I did little things you might see on a horror film. I put a large, black "X" through each of the pictures featured on the front of my cards. I also put the date and time of my *supposed* suicide on each card. I had tried very hard to make everything look as psycho and weird as I could. I wanted them to think I was completely looped and so out of my mind that I *really* would kill myself.

Being the good-natured nice guy that I am, I normally wouldn't have tried to play such a nasty joke on anyone – especially my relatives. However, I reasoned that sometimes you just gotta do what you gotta do if you want people to wake up and recognize your need to be taken care of.

When I called back 10 minutes later, the concerned tone of Anna's voice told me that my plan was working! I laughed to myself as I thought of how gullible Anna was. I wouldn't *really* kill myself! All I was trying to do was send a clear message – "I feel very unloved and very alone, and just want someone to give me the love and attention I need."

Interrupting Anna, I asked to speak to my sister-in-law, Megan. But within a few seconds Anna came back on the line and said that Megan refused to speak to me. After asking to speak to Derek, she explained that he, too, refused. In fact, she angrily explained, nobody was willing to talk to me – they were all too scared. When I asked what they were scared *of*, she loudly replied – "YOU!!"

CHAPTER 4

Putting My Plan Into Action

As Anna left the phone again, I was pleased to hear frequent, fearful screaming in the background. As I thought about what to do next, I decided it was time to just lay it on the line with Anna. After all, it was nearly 11:30 on New Year's Eve and I was getting really tired of waiting for someone to come and rescue me. Besides, I needed someone to come fast - so that I wouldn't miss the fireworks display at midnight!

After waiting for what seemed like hours, I was elated when 21-year-old Cam Fletcher got on the phone. He was a young, kind, sincere person, whom I was sure would care whether I lived or died. I knew I could count on him.

"Cam," I explained, "Your mission - if you choose to accept it - is to get Megan into her SUV, begin driving down I-95 towards Las Vegas, and meet me before midnight. If you make it before midnight, you will save the day!"

"What do you mean?" Cam enquired.

"You will prevent me from killing myself," I calmly replied.

"And if I don't?" Cam asked in a very subdued tone.

"If you don't, I will be forced to commit suicide by driving my car the wrong way on the freeway and having a head on collision with the largest semi-truck I can find. Now, this is your mission! Do you accept?!!"

"I accept! I accept!" Cam shouted. "Just give us some time, Dave. We'll be there for you, buddy. Don't do anything stupid!"

"Thanks, Cam, I know I can count on you. And I *do* know what I'm doing. God bless you for helping me. I really hope to see you before midnight. If not, I'm sure you will see me in the next life." And with that, I hung up the phone.

Smiling to myself as I thought about Cam's willingness to rescue me, I hopped back into my car and began driving the short distance from the gas station back up to Derek and Anna's house.

As I neared the house I quickly turned left, headed east up a short street, turned left again, then backed the car up behind a large tree (This move would prevent anyone inside the house from discovering my position). As I quietly turned off the car I eagerly anticipated the moment Megan and Cam would come rushing out of the house and squeal out of the driveway on their way to find me and save my life. When they did drive off, I would follow them, being careful not to be detected. Then, at precisely 11:59 p.m., as they frantically raced down I-95 searching for me, I would flash my lights, pass them, and get them to pull over. I would also ensure I credited *them* with "saving" my life. Thinking *they* had accomplished such a great thing, they would probably cry and want to hug me and tell me how glad they were that I was still alive. In short, they would give me all the attention I needed.

Much to my surprise, however, as the minutes slowly ticked away *nobody – not even Cam* - came rushing out of the house to save me! Just in case they were running behind, I waited until 12:30. But realizing that my hope was in vain, I decided they had failed the *ultimate* test. They had totally let me down when I needed them most.

Shrugging off my disappointment and knowing that in their minds

I no longer existed, I resolved to keep a positive attitude. I would start a new life for myself somewhere south of Utah in a place where nobody would know me or have a clue about my pregnant wife and two young children or my history of Mental Illness.

CHAPTER 5

The Search for Jessica Simpson

Over the next few hours I thought a lot about my children. I loved them *so* much. While everyone else I knew hated me, it was comforting to know that *they* still loved and cared for me. It had been so hard for me to leave them. But when Aimee adamantly told me I couldn't take them with me to Utah, I decided I'd better listen.

Although I didn't want to be without them – my best friends – I knew that taking them would only mean that Aimee would call the cops and try to convince them I was a psychotic kidnapper.

• • •

The next day I found myself parked outside the Salt Lake City Airport with a plan to take a plane to Las Vegas. If all went as planned, I felt sure I could meet up with my newly discovered idol - Jessica Simpson. In an article I had recently read about her, I discovered that she was looking for a husband. The article even described the qualities she wanted in her husband, and much to my humble surprise, I had *every* single one!

Feeling somewhat discouraged about the likelihood of *The* Jessica Simpson falling for me – a married man with a history of mental problems – I took courage when I remembered that Billy Joel had once spent time in a mental institution. Apparently it was there that he resolved to really live life to the fullest, and decided that he wanted to use his talents to become famous. He also resolved to marry a beautiful woman. Not long after that, he *did* become famous and married an undeniably gorgeous Super Model - Christie Brinkley. I reasoned that if Billy Joel could do it, so could I! For all I knew, maybe I too, was destined to marry a beautiful, famous woman and have gorgeous little children with her!

As I watched the flight times on the T.V. monitors, I noticed that the next scheduled flight to Las Vegas, which was supposed to leave in two hours, had been cancelled. Unsure about what to do next, a plan quickly came to my mind. I would rent a car from the airport and *drive* to Las Vegas. By driving, not only would I avoid security screening and the possibility that someone would think I was a "nut case," but I would also have a way to get around the city while I searched for my new true love.

After renting a car, I decided it was time to go "underground." As far as my friends and family were concerned, I was dead. That being the case, I felt very peaceful knowing that I was free from all the stress, expectations, and responsibilities I had had only hours earlier.

Wanting to get rid of all evidence of my "former life," I destroyed my driver's license and my blood donor card and threw them into the garbage. Next, I chucked my video rental card, followed by my tanning card and finally my library card. Knowing I would need the cash available on my two credit cards, I decided to save them, and at some point in time make a single, huge withdrawal of cash. That way nobody would be able to track my purchases. Lastly, I thought about ripping up an important church document I carried in my wallet. Hesitating for a few moments, I decided that if my identity was going to be kept a secret, I would have to break all ties with my church. Staring at the small driver's-license-sized piece of paper wrapped in clear plastic, I debated for another minute, then pulled it out of it's case, tore it into tiny pieces, and when nobody was watching, quickly but discreetly threw it into the garbage with everything else.

At that moment I decided it was time – just for a little while – to experience what the *other* side of life was like!

CHAPTER 6

_____

Assuming My New Identity

S tepping into my brand new Pontiac Grand Prix, I felt like a new man. Instead of my rusty 1986 Honda Accord, I would begin my quest to marry Jessica Simpson in style. As I pulled away, I whispered goodbye to Derek and Anna and Megan and put all thoughts of contacting them - to let them know I was alive - out of my mind. I reasoned that telling them my plans would only be continuing to burden them with my problems – something I was now convinced they wanted no part of.

Driving through numerous construction zones, I headed in what I thought was a southerly direction as I looked for signs that would point the way to Las Vegas – or Sin City - as the Jessica Simpson article had called it. Now that I had destroyed virtually everything that would iden- tify me for who I really was, I began to feel a freedom I had never felt before. Being anonymous felt wonderful. Nobody I knew would ever find out what I was up to. After finding I-80, I headed west and slammed the accelerator of my fancy sports car to the floor. As it jumped forward, all thoughts of my old life left my mind.

After about half an hour I began to feel very sleepy. But despite the strong urge to pull over, I kept driving. I cranked up the air conditioning, blasted the stereo, and pulled out the magazine I had purchased days earlier in Montana, the cover of which featured a picture of my gorgeous, blonde-haired, blue-eyed wife to be.

In an attempt to stay awake, and also wanting to practice what I would say when I found her, I put Jessica's picture in the middle of the steering wheel, and began having an imaginary conversation with her. From the way she looked, and from what I had read, she seemed like a really nice, talented, head-screwed-on-straight kind of woman. That being the case, I was confident she would be interested in me – a man who was all those things and more.

After driving for what *seemed* like hours, and barely being able to keep my eyes open, I decided to stop. After all, it wasn't worth risking my life just to get to Las Vegas right away. I pulled into a small town to find a place to sleep for the night.

As I entered the town I was shocked! Wendover, Nevada was a town unlike any I had ever seen! It was just one long road of colorful, bright, inviting casinos, all of which begged for my attention.

Ignoring my exhaustion, I located the biggest, brightest hotel in town and checked myself in. My room had a full-size Jacuzzi tub and two king-sized beds! I forced myself to lay down to get some desperately needed sleep, but try as I might, all I could think about was Jessica. Jessica, Jessica, Jessica.

CHAPTER 7

Continuing My Quest for Jessica

I kept rolling the image of *The* Jessica Simpson around and around and around in my mind. Sleep became unimportant compared to the prospect of proposing to my new sweetheart.

Feeling discouraged at the prospect of finding her in the huge city of Las Vegas, and not knowing what to do next, a perfect plan came to my mind! I could contact her by phone from my hotel room! And even though the chances of her number being listed in the Las Vegas phone directory were slim, I decided it wouldn't hurt to try. I quickly hopped off the bed, started filling the hot-tub with water, and grabbed the phone.

After grabbing my P.D.A. to enter her number, I gently eased into the tub and made my first call to Directory Assistance. An hour and a half later I had the number of every Jessica or "J." Simpson listed in Las Vegas. None of them, however, were *The* Jessica Simpson.

Remembering that I still had not made my HUGE withdrawal of cash, I jumped out of the hot tub, dried off, put on my clothes, and headed downstairs to the bank machine. Using my bank card I pulled out all the cash our joint bank account had - $750.

Realizing that a mere $750 wouldn't buy me what I needed to start my new life, I decided to make one large credit card purchase - at just one store. After that, I would not be able to be tracked any further.

Even though it was 2 a.m. and I hadn't slept at all for over 24 hours, I decided to drive to the nearest store and spend, spend, spend. If I recalled correctly, I was pretty sure that my credit limit would allow me $4,000 worth of pure purchasing pleasure.

Once inside the store, I gathered up CD's, cologne, a radar detector, a television and stereo, new underwear and clothes, videos, and various other things I believed I would need to start my "new" life. But when the purchase didn't go through, I knew instantly that my "former" wife, Aimee, was behind it!

Angrily, I called the credit card company and *demanded* to know what was going on. Explaining that the matter was confidential, the man on the other end of the phone said there was nothing he could do. But I knew what was going on. After telling him I knew that Aimee had told them I was insane, I calmly convinced him that I was, in fact, Mentally Well. I further convinced him that Aimee was just a bitter wife, jealous that I had left her for another woman. A few minutes later the clerk tried my $3,900 purchase again. Much to my delight, this time it went through!

As I loaded the car with all my new stuff, I began to feel alone and decided it was time to find someone – anyone – to discuss my problems with. Back inside the casino, I tried to convince a 16-year-old girl behind the snack bar counter to listen.

Strangely, the more we talked, the more I forgot about Jessica and began to wonder if this was the girl who could give me the love and attention I was looking for. After a few minutes, however, my bubble burst when she declined my offer to take her out on a date after work.

Disappointed, I ignored my feelings of discouragement, realizing that her rejection only meant I would be able to re-focus my mind on finding Jessica. But as my rational mind began to kick in again for just a few moments, I began to feel as if my "quest" was hopeless and I decided to go outside for some fresh air. I ended up walking to another huge casino and wandered around for an hour trying to figure out what to do next. As I wondered what to do, some type of reality began to set in. Not only did I have nobody to talk to, but I was short on cash, hundreds of miles from home, and feeling more alone with each passing minute. On top of that, I was struck by the stark realization that since everyone *thought* I was dead, if I *really did* die here – maybe from starvation – nobody would know! Ignoring what I recognized as irrational fear, I continued to wander up and down the endless rows of slot machines.

Then, to my absolute surprise, I spotted a familiar-looking woman off in the distance. Even though her back was facing me she seemed to have some kind of familiarity. While I couldn't put my finger on it, I wondered if maybe it was someone I had gone to high school with. Or worse, maybe it was someone I knew from church – someone who would now find out that I was not really the sweet, innocent guy I had always tried to be - until now.

As I came closer, the woman's gorgeous blonde hair seemed to hang from her head like locks of gold. It was hard not to notice her hourglass figure and the poise and posture of confidence that seemed to radiate from her like an intense light. Then, as if I was in some kind of wonderful dream, she turned around and looked me straight in the eye. I couldn't believe my eyes!!

"Get outta here," I whispered to myself under my breath. "I really must be dreaming...this *can't* really be happening!"

CHAPTER 8

The REAL Jessica

As I listened to the unfamiliar noises coming from all over the casino, I was still in awe. My most incredible dream had come true. Only a few days earlier, I had not even known her name. But now, here I was, watching intently as she played the slot machines. Not only was she beautiful, but she was obviously very smart. I noticed that she had taken extra precautions to ensure nobody – especially the media – found out where she was. Her bodyguard and I were the only ones who shared her secret.

She was a beautiful blue-eyed, blonde-haired, gorgeous and famous woman, one who rarely went out in public undisguised for fear of having to sign thousands of autographs. The daughter of a preacher, the article I read had explained, Jessica was careful about who she hung out with and what she did. In fact, the writer of the article had pointed out, unlike most famous singer/supermodels who graced the cover of magazines, she was adamant about holding true to her Christian values. Though not the son of a preacher, I *also* came from a family who raised me with strict morals and Christian values. In short – we were made for each other!

After casually chatting for a few minutes, I asked Jessica if I could rest my head on her shoulder. Assuring her bodyguard it was okay, she willingly agreed. As I relaxed, all I could think about was how happy I was that I had finally found her, and how happy I would make Jessica if she accepted my proposal of marriage – an offer I would make when the time was right.

For several hours, I continued to rest my head on her shoulder. My arm now around her waist. I thought for a moment about the implications of what I was doing. Only a few days before I had never even darkened the door of a casino, much less hit on a woman other than my wife. Now I even had plans to ask her to marry me!

The clock slowly ticked past 2, then 3 a.m. It was almost 4 o'clock when I began to realize that, famous and stunningly gorgeous or not, Jessica Simpson had an addiction to gambling!

Although I pleaded with her with all the conviction and energy I had, she kindly refused my pleading to stop wasting money and get some sleep. She just kept pulling out more and more cash. When that ran out, she went to the main counter and asked for a safe to be opened so she could access even more money! My quick mental tally told me she was spending over $1,000 an hour, a price I knew she could afford, but not one that made any sense – especially at 4 a.m.!

Along with my concern about Jessica's gambling addiction, I began to feel annoyed that she would not shed her disguise in order for me to see her as she *really* was. Her coffee-stained, crooked teeth were a very effective disguise, but I was beginning to wonder if she really was *The* Jessica Simpson I thought she was. While her attractive female features were exactly the same as those I had seen in the magazine, the more I got to know her, the more she seemed different than what I expected she would be.

Deciding that for her own good I had to take action, I stopped her after a short bathroom break as she walked back to play the slot machines. After embracing for a moment, I lovingly asked her to reconsider what she was doing and stop gambling for the night. She replied that she couldn't. She simply had an addiction and was dealing with it in the only way she knew how. Then she said something that shocked me.

CHAPTER 9

Jessica Confesses

J essica explained that her husband had recently found out about her gambling addiction. (Husband?!!) She said he hated her for being so irresponsible and for wasting so much money. On top of it all, he announced that he was so angry he had decided to file for divorce. The worst part, she explained, was that everything her husband felt — his rage, his anger, his disappointment with her — were the same feelings she had about herself. She hated herself for what she was doing and the fact that she couldn't quit. Then, in a softer, quieter tone, she calmly revealed a secret, one which she said she had not shared with anyone else.

She explained that, although her life was a mess, she had a plan to make everything better. Once she ran out of money, and with nothing left to live for, she would commit suicide. That way, she explained, she would no longer have to deal with her husband, her gambling addiction, or her lack of money. And with that, she slowly began to walk back to the slot machines, with only $500 cash to spend before she would die.

Ordinarily, after that kind of deep discussion, I would have done everything in my power to suggest that suicide was not a smart idea. I would have tried with all my heart to convince her that her life *was* worth living, and that she was a wonderful and beautiful and loved person, regardless of how she felt. I also would have tried to persuade her to check herself into a mental institution where she would be safe.

The reality was, however, that my brain was definitely not functioning normally, and I felt incapable of doing any of that. On top of that I was stunned and shocked that Jessica was already married. How could the article I read have been wrong about that?! I was also shocked that such a beautiful, intelligent, successful woman could even think about killing herself! Slowly, I was beginning to realize that for the last four hours I had *not* been snuggling up to a Supermodel in disguise. Instead, I had been coming on to a middle-aged gambling addict whom I was sure was ready to make good on her promise of taking her own life.

• • •

Note: At this point, while I did not fully comprehend how "off-base" my thinking was, at the deepest level, I knew I was in desperate need of mental help. During the days that followed, I experienced brief moments of rational thought and correct perception. When not obvious, these moments are shown in italics to make it easier to understand.

• • •

CHAPTER 10

Reality Check

S aying nothing, I walked out right past the woman I was sure, only a few minutes earlier, was my "true love". Without even looking back at Jessica – or whatever her name was – I walked over to a payphone to call for help. As I did, a strange feeling came over me and I began asking myself some hard questions. Did I really believe that starting a relationship with this woman would be the answer to all my problems? What was I doing leaving my pregnant wife and two young children at home while I sat in a casino - with another woman - in Nevada? What am I going to do now that everyone thinks I'm dead?!

I felt scared and completely helpless. I knew I needed to call Aimee, explain what I had done, beg her forgiveness, and ask her to come rescue me. Through nearly seven years of marriage she had stuck with me, and I was hopeful that she would be able to tell me what to do to solve my problems and help me figure out how to get home. I was also hopeful that she wanted me back.

As I dialed my calling card number I silently prayed that Aimee would not hate me for leaving her and trying to find another woman. I hoped that somehow she would simply understand that I was not my normal self. While I believe that God heard my prayers, I guess he decided that Aimee had had about enough of me at that point. Try as I might, over and over again, the phone rang busy. Reaching a point of desperation I had never before felt in my life, I just stood there, immobilized by my fear. I knew I needed mental help in a very big way and I needed it now, before my rational mind completely exploded.

Not knowing what else to do, I slowly stumbled through the endless rows of slot machines to the front desk of the hotel. I began to gently sob, and with tears running down my cheeks, I slowly explained my situation to the woman behind the counter. I told her that I had no cash, no credit, no car, no nothing. Then, not caring what she thought of me, and wanting to emphasize how desperately I needed help, I also admitted that I had a history of mental problems. I further explained that I hadn't slept in over three days. I told her that I knew I would be okay if I could just sleep — somewhere. Barely able to understand me as I cried, the woman continued to listen, while at the same time casually motioning to a security guard that she needed help.

After requesting they contact someone from my church so I could be properly taken care of, the large, gentle security guard escorted me to a room where I could wait until someone figured out what to do. Stopping for a moment, I remembered "Jessica" and her plans to commit suicide. I told the security guard, who radioed his partner, who assured me he would do what he could.

CHAPTER 11

What Really Happened

L aying on the soft chair of the hotel waiting room all I could think about was the regret and shame I felt. I was a true idiot, low-life, jerk, deadbeat Dad, hopeless husband. You name it, I felt it. What on earth was I doing? Why could I not see how much Aimee loved me? After all, during my most recent hospitalization she visited me every day for the three weeks I spent in hospital. She even wore makeup and perfume, something she knew I loved. Why had I taken her for granted? Even after learning I was a Mentally Ill low-life, she had made the decision to stick with me, despite my emotional instability and irritability.

But why did she decide to stick with me when so many of our friends and acquaintances had divorced after finding out their spouses had a Mental Illness? What did she see in me that was worth loving? How could she forgive what I had done in the past? Even worse, I wondered if this time maybe she would see past the wonderful person she *thought* I was and look deep down inside. Maybe *this* time she would see that I *really was* nothing more than an emotionally unstable, Mentally Ill idiot who would never be able to support his family or be a decent father.

As these questions swirled around in my mind the woman from the front desk came into the room to let me know that an official from my church *was* willing to come and help but would not arrive for two hours. Disappointed, I again closed my eyes and tried desperately to fall asleep.

Unable to rest, however, my mind turned next to the family I grew up in. Regardless of the emotionally charged "issues" I had with my parents, I loved Mom and Dad and all my siblings dearly. I thought of the comforting words my mother spoke so often to me as a child and later as a teenager. She had always told me that she and Dad "would love me no matter what." As I pondered on that thought, I decided that what I was doing now would be a real big test of that unconditional love.

• • •

As I concentrated on slowing down my accelerated thinking and focused on how to contact Aimee, I felt as if as if a guardian angel was whispering in my ear. With what little ability for rational thought I had left, through the foggy corridors of my mind, I could envision my Dad in a small hotel on the other side of... Wendover?!

As I struggled to concentrate, I remembered that *he actually was in Wendover!* In fact, I recalled, I had had dinner with him at a different Casino two nights earlier. During dinner he had explained that he had cancelled all the appointments at his busy legal practice and had caught the first plane to Salt Lake to "rescue" me. At the time, however, not wanting him to persuade me to come home, I had ditched him.

Almost chalking it up to another delusion, I was shocked when I realized I had been in Wendover for over three days. My Dad really was in Wendover, Nevada, staying at a motel not more than a mile away. I really did have dinner with him two days earlier. Why I ran away remained a mystery to me, but just knowing he was there to protect me brought comfort to my soul.

I quickly sat up in my chair and explained to the security guard that, although I was "out of it," I was sure that my father was staying in town.

After giving him Dad's name and location, he called to find out if what I was saying was really true. I hoped and prayed it was.

CHAPTER 12

Dad to the Rescue

To everyone's surprise - including my own - Dad was staying at a
hotel in Wendover. After a brief pause, the person on the other end of
the phone said he would be right over.

As I eagerly anticipated his arrival, my thoughts turned to my childhood and my relationship with my father.

Dad and I had not always been the best of friends. I resented his
attempts to control me and I think he resented my attempts to resist.
On the positive side, however, I made many wise decisions when I was
growing up in an effort to do what Dad (and Mom) wanted.

However, at this point, having spent a good portion of the night
coming on to a woman I believed was a famous Super Model I thought
I was destined to marry, I knew things wouldn't go over real well with
Dad. And, despite the fact that I was quickly approaching my 30's, I was
still very concerned about what he would think of me. However, at that
point I really, really, did not care. I knew Dad loved me and would take
care of me. He would let me stay in his hotel room and get the sleep my
body and mind were now craving.

As Dad walked in the door, the sight of his familiar face brought tears
to my eyes as a feeling of complete relief washed over me. Here was
an honest, hard-working father who had left his legal practice to come
rescue his son at a time of dire need. I hugged him, told him that I loved

him, and thanked him for coming to get me. After assuring me that everything would be okay, and that he loved me too, we drove to a small hotel without a casino (one of the only ones of its kind in Wendover), where Dad already had a bed waiting for me. As he laid down on his bed, while I laid down on mine, he said something about being glad that he found me, as I slowly – almost – began to drift off to sleep.

CHAPTER 13

Mom Reveals Jessica's Real Location

S trangely, however, I again found it impossible to sleep and asked Dad if he thought it would be okay if I called Mom – just to let her know how I was doing. He replied that he would prefer for me to get some sleep first, but that if I really needed to I could go use the payphone in the lobby. As I left the room I began to sob like a baby as I thought about how comforting it was to be in the trusted care of my father.

After accepting my collect call, Mom sounded tired but happy to hear my voice as I began explaining my story to her. Knowing she would have a soft spot in her heart for the fact that I had *almost* found my true love, I told her all the details. Then, to my complete surprise, my mother revealed to me that she already knew that Jessica Simpson was not in Nevada. When I asked how, she said it was because she was in a small town in Idaho waiting to meet up with me! She explained that I was right about the fact that she was traveling in disguise. But apparently, the *real* Jessica Simpson had flown her jet helicopter to this small Idaho town – in the middle of the night – to avoid being noticed by the public. She also said that Jessica was anxious to meet me. When I asked how Jessica would even know about me, she explained that one of my numerous voice-mail messages had gotten through to her. Not being able to contact me, Jessica somehow ended up contacting Mom and told her she wanted to meet up with me in Idaho!

Shocked by my good fortune I started bawling like a baby and, in a shaky voice, I asked, "Mom, are you *sure* she's really there – and that she's waiting for *me*?"

"She really is son. I wouldn't lie to you," Mom explained quietly. "But you need to get your father, get packed up, and leave immediately. She is a very wealthy woman and time is money to her. You don't want to keep her waiting any longer than you have to."

"Thanks, Mom," I sobbed.

"You're welcome son. Now make sure to go wake your father right now so that you don't keep her waiting, okay son?"

"Okay, Mom. I love you."

"I love you too, son."

And with that we said goodbye to each other.

Still in shock that my *own mother* was supporting me in leaving my wife and children, I was even more surprised that she had actually arranged for me to meet Jessica Simpson. Somewhat confused, I continued to try and wrap my head around what was happening.

But as I thought more and more about it, something just didn't sit right with me. The simple fact was, my mother was the type of person who normally would have spent hours pleading with me to *forget* Jessica and return home to Aimee.

And then it came to me. I shook my head and laughed to myself as I realized that Mom had almost succeeded in deceiving me.

Thinking back to our conversation, she had played her game fairly well. But remembering the condescending tone of voice she used while talking to me, she thought I was in the middle of another manic episode and was so "out of it" that I would actually believe her lie. The truth was, she was completely uninterested in my quest to find Jessica. Instead, she knew that if she tricked me into going to

Idaho, my Dad's cousin, a doctor, would be able to inject me with "anti-psychotic" medication

"Man," I thought to myself, "She must really think I'm stupid."

Without going back to Dad's hotel room, I decided that I was wrong to want to go back to Aimee and our children. I rationalized that doing so would only be subjecting myself to more arguments with my parents about the way I should live my life. Not only would I have to listen to *their* opinions, but I knew Aimee would be right there with them, constantly reminding me of the need to become a more responsible, stable husband and father.

In an effort to put off dealing with what I was sure would amount to major psychological trauma, I calmly walked outside and then ran as fast as I could, hiding in the bathroom of one of the casinos.

Exactly what happened next is not completely clear in my mind. In the end, however, Dad found me and persuaded me, against my will, to travel back to Salt Lake City. We agreed that if the hospital confirmed that my Mental State was okay, he would leave me alone to do whatever I wanted.

CHAPTER 14

Inspiration from God

As we neared our destination, my desire to keep my commitment of going to the hospital for assessment began to dwindle and I began to feel as if God was leading me in a different direction. Although my father begged me to come with him to the hospital, he slammed on the brakes when he realized that my threat to jump out was real. As soon as he stopped, I jumped out of the car and ran as fast as my legs would take me. After hiding behind a nearby building for several minutes, I decided that Dad would probably assume that I had kept running and would likely be looking for me several blocks away.

Looking around, I found myself near Temple Square in downtown Salt Lake City. As I surveyed the area and thought about what to do next, I felt compelled to enter the huge Conference Center of my church, The Church of Jesus Christ of Latter-Day Saints.

After completing a tour, I felt impressed to speak to a very beautiful young woman who had also been on the tour. As I walked toward her, intent on discussing my feelings with her, I was blocked by a large, middle-aged man in a dark suit. The man kindly introduced himself and asked if I would be willing to sit down and chat with him.

Chat with him? Of course I would! During the tour I had had many strong feelings about the need to warn the Church leaders in Salt Lake about dangers they were unaware of and how people would try to take their lives. I also felt strongly that they needed to know that God wanted me to join them in leading the Church in Salt Lake!

Once inside a private room, the man began speaking to me in a very kind, warm tone of voice. I sensed that he was a man of God and had no doubt that he had crucial information for me. But instead of discussing the affairs of the Church, he asked if I would be willing to change my mind about going to the hospital with my father. Puzzled at how he would even know my father, I replied that I *would* be willing to go, but that I would only feel comfortable going with *him*. With a concerned half-smile on his face, the gentle man consented to take me.

We left the room, and after picking up his wife from another part of the large building, we hopped in their luxury sedan and headed for the University of Utah hospital. After ensuring that I was looked after, the man patted me on the back and left.

Entrusted to the care of a kind (and good looking) nurse, I willingly consented to receive a needle - in the butt! Moments later, I was falling into a deep, peaceful sleep.

CHAPTER 15

_____

Waking Up

N ow, I don't know about you, but I was not used to falling asleep in one place and waking up in another. So when I woke up in the parking lot of a Great Falls, Montana gas station, I was one confused, scared little man. On top of being many more hours from Las Vegas and Jessica, my Dad, who was now adamant that I remain in the car, was still under the impression that I was going to go back to Canada with him!

I reminded him several times that I had only consented to go home if the doctors in Utah thought I had a problem. He pointed out that the doctor's *did* think I had a problem and had given me the needle in the butt to help slow me down. I corrected him by letting him know what the nurse had said. I didn't actually have a problem, but just needed a shot to calm my nerves. "In fact," I explained, "In light of all the stress I had been under, *she* thought I was acting completely normal!"

Despite my pleadings, and true to his old controlling nature, Dad *insisted* I stay in the car and come home with him. When I pressed him, he admitted that he *did* have plans to take me to another hospital just north of the Canadian border. He did say, however, that if the doctors *there* said I was okay, he would let me go.

"Alright, Dad," I said, "I have had enough! Let's examine the situation at this point: Mom thinks I'm dumb enough to believe that Jessica

Simpson was waiting for me in Idaho. After lying to me once to get me to the hospital, you are lying to me again, and you think I am stupid enough to believe you! On top of it all, you *and* Mom both seem to think I have some kind of mental problem!!! Why can't you see that I am just fed up with my crappy job, my crappy marriage, my crappy controlling parents, my crappy car, my crappy rented duplex, and my crappy, always negative balance in my crappy bank account!!!!! Yes, I'm feeling a little stressed, but don't try to get me to go back to my wife by lying to me!!"

With that, as he noticed I was almost ready to bolt from the car, Dad said, "Wait! Your friends are here!"

CHAPTER 16

Stabbed in the Back by my Best Friends

" Friends?!" I said, perplexed.

"Yes, Nick and Darryl were concerned about you. They both took time off work to make the six hour trip to Great Falls. If you don't believe me, look inside the window of the gas station."

To my surprise, he was right! There – in Great Falls, Montana of all places, were my two best friends in the whole wide world.

As they came out of the gas station I felt a little ashamed of what I was doing. I realized that they probably had not known about the marriage problems Aimee and I had been experiencing for the past several years.

"Hey Dave!" they said in unison as they jumped in the car.

"Hey, guys! What are you doing here?"

They explained that my mother (whom we all agreed worries a lot) had asked if they would be willing to travel to Montana to see if there was anything they could help with. I explained that while I was grateful they had traveled so far to give me support, they just would not understand why I felt so strongly about not going back to Aimee. I further explained that, contrary to what my mother said, I did *not* have a mental problem, but was just trying to escape my stressful life. I also told them I had decided to make Nevada my new home.

I thought they would understand, but to my surprise, they *both* tried to talk me into going back to Aimee. Just as I had once been deceived into thinking, they thought that she was a pretty decent person. After explaining my reasons for not wanting to go back, and recognizing that both Nick and Darryl didn't believe me, but had been sucked in by Mom and Dad's lies, I decided it was high time to escape to freedom.

As I lunged toward the door handle Nick smacked the lock down and grabbed me. Holding me tight he explained through clenched teeth that forcing me to go back to Canada was for my own good, and that I needed help. "Yea, right," I thought to myself. Then I bit his finger, smacked him in the face with the back of my head, popped the lock up, flung open the door, and ran as fast as my legs would take me. I ran and ran and ran until I was satisfied that Nick and Darryl and my Dad would never be able to find me or attempt to ruin my life plans ever again.

CHAPTER 17

_____

Safe in the Comfort of the Hospital

L onely, cold and afraid, and knowing that the last two people
on earth I could call my friends had turned against me, I was
in complete and utter despair. As I walked through a middle-
income residential neighborhood the thought of stealing a car crossed
my mind. Even though I had no idea how to go about it, I knew that
doing so would allow me to start driving back south and continue my
quest to find Jessica. However, not wanting to get in trouble with the
law, I quickly decided against it, knowing that the Lord would take care
of me – somehow.

As I wandered aimlessly, the bright headlights of a passing car lit up
the parking lot of an abandoned gas station and I found myself considering the possibility of spending the night there. But the thought quickly
left my mind as I realized the car was a police cruiser!

As the car stopped and the female officer exited, I felt almost relieved.
The attractive officer had obviously been alerted that there was a "loony
on the loose," and in a town the size of Great Falls, it had been easy for
her to find me. Not having broken the law, but simply having abandoned
my two-faced friends, I was sure the kind woman would take care of me
and find a warm place for me to stay – even if she had to put me up in
a hotel for the night.

After confirming that I was the David Grant Miller she was looking for, she invited me to sit in the hardened plastic back seat of the police cruiser. While it was not comfortable, it was much warmer than the cool January air. I felt a sense of relief knowing that I was in the hands of someone I could trust.

After answering several questions obviously aimed at determining whether I had a mental problem, the officer kindly suggested that, since I had no money and no place to stay for the night, I could at least go to the hospital. There, she explained, they would provide a warm bed and a few warm meals. And, if they decided nothing was wrong with me, I would be free to leave. Feeling strongly that I should trust this particular officer, I agreed, realizing there would be no harm in just getting a simple assessment.

• • •

I don't remember much about being admitted to the hospital that night, except that I got another shot which enabled me to get the sleep my mind and body so desperately needed. In that warm, comfortable bed I felt safer, happier, and more contented than I had for weeks. Here, under the care of an attractive female doctor, I would at least be listened to and respected for who I was and not be judged on the moral correctness of leaving my wife and children in search of a better life.

After a quick assessment, the doctor kindly consented to my request to stay for a few days – just to relax and relieve all the stress I was feeling from everyone. It was a break I gladly welcomed. That's why I was a little surprised and extremely disappointed when my *mother* showed up!

When she walked in the room and began casually chatting, I knew she was up to no good. After realizing why she was being so nice, I flatly refused the herbal supplements she had smuggled into the hospital in her purse, and immediately alerted the nurse to what she was doing. Realizing she was caught, Mom explained the history of the herbal supplement and its success in the treatment of people with big-time mental problems. But despite the nurse's okay for Mom to go ahead and give me the supplement, I refused. Instead, I decided not to talk to my mother and requested that the nurses show her out. I explained that I was trying to get a break from all the stress I felt, and that I would only be able to accomplish my goal without the presence of my mother – one of the main sources of my stress in the first place!

The last thing I remember of the mental hospital in Great Falls is covering my body in shaving cream and trying to walk out unnoticed. After being pinned down by several male nurses, however, I felt a familiar poke in the behind.

The next thing I remember is waking up in the back seat of my rusty 1986 Honda Accord with *Aimee* by my side!! While her Dad listened as he drove, she explained to me that we were heading north and were just a few miles south of the Canada/U.S. border. She told me that now that I was awake, I would need to be quiet and act "normal" as we crossed the border.

Thinking I was having some kind of anti-psychotic drug-induced hallucination, I thrashed around the inside of the car trying to unlock the door and jump out. But thrash as I might, and despite her big, eight-month-pregnant, basketball-shaped tummy, my "hallucination" held me even tighter than Nick had a few nights before. As her fingernails began to dig into my skin, Aimee's angry voice became more and more real with each passing second.

When we came to the border, I was sure I could persuade the guard that I was being kidnapped by my own wife and taken against my will to Canada. But despite my pleadings and explanations that I was just "sowing my wild oats", the guard seemed to have little sympathy for me, nor a desire to arrest Aimee for kidnapping! Instead, he seemed like he was biting his tongue to stop himself from laughing or something.

Trying hard to be stern he waved us through, not even acknowledging the crime Aimee was committing!! As we traveled for another 45 minutes toward the small southern Canadian town of Lethbridge, Alberta, my heart sank.

CHAPTER 18

Guilty As Charged

M y wife, Aimee, had won. Mom had won. Dad had won. Nick and Darryl had won. Derek and Anna had won. Megan had won. I was the *only* loser in the huge game they were playing – the game of trying to get me to fall in love and get back together with Aimee, *after* I got medical treatment for what they all *thought* was an out-of-control Mental Illness.

Realizing I had lost, I reluctantly agreed to go with Aimee into the Psych Ward of the local hospital. In return, Aimee agreed to let me go free, but only if the doctor's assessment revealed that I was *not* in the middle of a severe, out of control, manic episode.

• • •

Sadly, and to my disgust, I just happened to get a psychiatrist who was easily swayed. Aimee, her father, and later my father *all* expressed their bogus concerns to the doctor – and he bought the whole story – hook, line and sinker!! I watched with horror as the gullible doctor signed the order for me to stay. All I could do was shake my head and feel sorry for him because of his lack of ability to do what *he* thought was right. Realizing I was beat, I stood up, politely shook the spineless doctor's hand, and asked where my room was. Despite my reservations of being forcibly confined, I decided I might as well look on the bright side. I would have my own warm room, a comfortable bed, a hot shower, and the opportunity to flirt with several gorgeous student nurses!!!

I was dreaming about all the fun I would have when I was jolted back to reality by my mother's voice. It seemed that she and Dad were having some kind of an argument with the doctor regarding my course of treatment. The doctor believed I needed a shot of "time-release" anti-psychotic medication to bring me down out of my *supposed* mania and back to reality. But my parents were concerned about the long term effects of injecting such a powerful drug into my medication-sensitive body. Instead, Mom suggested using the herbal supplement she had tried to sneak into the hospital in Great Falls. Both her and my father believed it would have the same powerful effect.

Realizing that my sometimes stubborn but loving mother and father were not going to back down easily, the doctor suggested the idea of holding an informal hospital court. With dignitaries from the community and outside psychiatric experts, it would be determined, in a democratic way, whether I would be forcibly injected with medication or if I would be allowed to opt for the natural alternative my parents believed in so strongly.

Somehow, the merits of the "democracy" the doctor spoke of seemed like a big load of medical B.S. when I took into consideration the fact that neither he, nor my parents had even thought to ask me what *I* wanted to do!! I was expected to just sit there and quietly smile while the battle for decisions regarding my life raged on.

Disgusted with the whole thing and wanting to relieve some stress, I decided to take a long, hot shower. Knowing the informal court session would not be held for several days, I decided to forget the whole thing – at least for now.

After getting dressed in my lovely, green, designer hospital outfit, I wandered out of my room to eat supper. After flirting with a few student nurses and even a few patients who obviously *did* have mental problems, I just sat silently and shook my head. All I could think about was how incompetent every medical professional on the unit was - a judgment based on the fact that they all seemed to believe that I *really did* have a mental problem. "Oh well", I thought. "They will eventually realize I am just a normal guy with an abnormal amount of stress!"

• • •

In the end, the court (heavily swayed by my spineless doctor and a two-faced nurse) found me guilty. I was "sentenced" to receive one shot in the butt, which, I was politely informed, would be for my best good. Though my mother and father were outraged, the judge told them to suck it up and move on. The judge then set the time for my injection (as is done for lethal injections in prison) at exactly 6pm that night. Ironically, even the "democratic" court had refused to listen to what *I* wanted to do. But then, that was the story of my life.

Maybe the reason nobody would listen to little old me - the one actually receiving the injection - was because what *I* wanted wouldn't please either side. I didn't want my injection, for fear it would make me sleep for weeks, causing me to miss the birth of our baby. But I was also strongly against the "herbal remedy" my parents were so sold on, fearing the side effects I had experienced once before.

• • •

At precisely 6 p.m., *six* male psych nurses entered the room! I began screaming and yelling in protest, begging them not to inject the "anti-psychotic" drug. Not even one of them had any sympathy for me! Like the rest of the medical people, they were all spineless robots - following orders without questioning the moral correctness of their actions. In just a few seconds I was down on the ground, my loose green hospital pants pulled halfway down my buttocks. A moment later, the needle had pierced my skin, injecting the strong anti-psychotic medication into my bloodstream.

Realizing I was beat, I stopped kicking, stopped screaming, and stopped my pleading. There was nothing I could do. Instead, I did what any gentleman would do - I shook the hands of all six nurses and thanked them for their time and for doing what they really believed was right — then sent them on their way.

CHAPTER 19

Getting Even

T his time the doctors and nurses had won. I was, again, the big loser in this terrible game that everyone was playing with me. As much as I had been scared that the shot would knock me out for weeks, as much as my parents had fought it, and as much as I had struggled, kicked, screamed, bit and punched to avoid getting my shot, it really didn't matter now. The deed was done and that was that. I had been violated – legally – without my consent and there wasn't a darn thing I could do about it now. Or was there?

Believing I only had about an hour before the medication would render me unconscious, I tried to think of something – anything – I could do to get back at the doctor who had ordered the shot. Running through my options I decided against trying to escape, rationalizing that more screaming and yelling wouldn't help. Then I remembered something I had learned in one of my college courses while working on my degree in Communications, about the powerful influence of the media. I had learned about what "made" the news and what did not, and I was pretty sure my ordeal was a juicy story that *definitely* would!

With only 40 minutes before the medication would literally knock me off my feet, I mentally reviewed the facts to ensure my "news story" would meet the media's criteria. Was it a topic that would be of interest to, or affect the public? Of course it was – one in five people are person-ally affected by a Mental Illness. The other four out of five are friends or relatives or co-workers.

Next, I asked myself if there was there anything unusual about the situation. Definitely! First, I didn't *actually* have a mental problem, and had been institutionalized against my will. Second, even after my parents successfully got a court order to stop the injection, it was *still* given. In fact, the administration of the medication was so unjust that I knew of one employee who had put his job on the line by refusing, on ethical grounds, to give the injection. Third, my wife was due to have our third child in days, and the doctors were well aware that the medication could knock me out for weeks, resulting in me missing the birth.

Becoming more and more excited, I knew that I *really did* have a juicy news story that any local TV station or newspaper would eat up! As I quickly but discreetly headed toward the psych ward public telephone, I couldn't wait to stick it to the doctors and the nurses by way of public embarrassment. When the story broke in this small city where everyone knows everybody – including the psych nurses and doctors - there was gonna be heck to pay!

Nonchalantly flipping through the yellow pages I quickly found the number for the news department of the largest T.V. station in town, dialed, and prepared for the short sales pitch I would need to give. My goal: to convince the news person to come to the hospital to investigate my story. I looked at the clock on the wall. It was 11 p.m. I knew that if I was convincing enough the station could do their research the next morning and air my red-hot story on the 5 o'clock news.

After a short five minute conversation with the news director, he assured me that I was right about my story being big and promised to send someone out the next morning to interview me. I politely thanked him, hung up the phone, and shouted for joy. These sons of guns weren't going to know what hit them!!!

CHAPTER 20

In the End, the Doctor Always Wins

The next morning I was abruptly awakened by a nurse who normally treated my very kindly. She demanded to know what was going on! Pretending not to know what she was referring to, she continued to shoot several pointed questions at me, aimed at getting me to confess that I called the TV station. But I wouldn't budge. I had exposed their scandal and they knew it and they were going to pay! By the time I got up out of bed for an emergency meeting with the doctor, I realized my plan had worked! Nurses were whispering to each other and looking at me, all with grave looks of concern on their faces. The best part was, even my stuck-up doctor looked as if his over-inflated ego had had a big, fat needle poked right in the middle of it!!

Knowing this was now *my* show, and that *everyone else* were now the losers, I firmly and rudely declined my doctor's demand to meet with him in private 'at once'. I stood my ground as he tried his best to intimidate me into doing what he wanted. In a loud voice (so the nurses that were within earshot could hear clearly) I explained *why* I refused to meet with him privately, citing his tendency to treat me with rudeness and disrespect when nobody else could hear. Looking somewhat embarrassed, he denied the claim. Speaking even louder, I gave an example of when he had made inappropriate and rude comments about my mother.

As he began to blush with embarrassment, he became adamant. He explained very firmly, and quite rudely, that *he* was the doctor and *I* was the patient, and that I had better do what he wanted. I responded with a polite, "Up Yours, doctor!" I knew my rights and I was well aware that unless I was exhibiting dangerous behavior, he could not *force* me to do anything.

Deciding it was hopeless to reason with me, he decided to give it to me as straight and rudely as he could. Looking around to ensure no nurses were within earshot, he lowered his voice almost to a whisper and said: "Look, David, this has become kind of like some surgeries – it is very messy... *very* messy. I don't know *why* you called the T.V. station, or how you ever convinced them to believe you, but I *refuse* to deal with this! I haven't wanted you here since the day you arrived and I certainly don't want you here now. So I am sending you back to Ponoka where *they* can deal with you!!" And with that, he turned and left.

True to his word, at 7:30 a.m. – only 15 minutes later – I was loaded in the back of an ambulance. With sirens screaming (as if there was some type of dire emergency), we sped to the airport where I was loaded into a small airplane used as an air ambulance. By 8:10 a.m. – less than an hour after my heated argument with the doctor – we were in the air. By 9:20 a.m., I was sitting in front of a male psychiatric nurse whose name I remembered from my last visit.

CHAPTER 21

My Stay at the Mental Hospital

After dutifully checking my pulse, blood pressure and breathing, John commented on how disappointed he was to see me again. He said that he had heard about all the weird stuff I had done down in the States, including my frivolous attempt to find and marry *The* Jessica Simpson. He also told me I was lucky to be alive. Then, in an effort to teach me a lesson, he reiterated to me the stupidity of my decision to go off the medication prescribed to me during my first hospital visit. He also gave a short dissertation on the insanity of pursuing a gorgeous Super Model with the purpose of proposing marriage, as well as the absurdity of trying to deal with my Mental Illness on my own. He further explained that I was one of the "lucky ones" because I responded well to medication and would be able to live a normal life. However, he adamantly continued, my "normal life" would only materialize if I would stop trying to be so independent and resign myself to the fact that I would only be normal *with* medication.

Not really wanting to listen to me, he interrupted when I tried to respond to his negative verbal barrage. In a matter-of-fact tone of voice, he asked me to count backwards from 100. Understanding that good behavior was my ticket to getting out of the hospital as soon as possible, I began - 100, 99, 98, 97. But to my surprise, he interrupted me again and told me I was doing it all wrong! He wanted me to count backwards by *sevens*! Now, I don't know about you, but I would have a hard time counting *backward* by *sevens* from *100* if I was sitting in a high school math class writing it down on a piece of paper! So, asking me to perform what I consider mental gymnastics at such a stressful time was, in my opinion, a little much. As I'm sure you can imagine, he didn't have much sympathy for my lack of ability to mentally calculate numbers. He marked something down on his chart indicating that I was not mentally stable enough to make what he thought was a very simple calculation. What a bozo!

CHAPTER 22

Meeting with the Doctor (and His Ego)

You know how in life there are some people you instantly click with? On the other hand, there are also people you just can't stand the sight of? Well, my doctor fit into the latter category, and I figure I probably did with him too. He was a no-nonsense, feelingless German, calloused from years of working with thousands of wing nuts whose brain power and capabilities were far below his superior intellect. Problem was, when he encountered someone who wasn't willing to feed his ego and treat him like God, he didn't take it very well. But, while I give him credit for not getting angry or upset like my doctor in the Psych Ward had done, he did, nonetheless, manifest his disgust, but in a much quieter, discreet and powerful way. He knew what I wanted and he knew he could eventually force even me to do anything to get it. Let me explain.

During our first of several meetings, I let Dr. Cromwell know that his plan to try and force me to take medication was flawed. Unlike all the other spineless, wimpy patients he was accustomed to dealing with, *I* would not budge – no matter what! I had made up my mind and there was no turning back. Citing a logical explanation for my position, I explained that, from past experience, I knew the pills he was trying to force on me made my head so foggy that I could barely think straight. I don't know about you, but to me that was just not a position I was willing to put myself in! On top of all that, I explained that I was also very familiar with the risks involved. Impressing him with my knowledge, I explained to Dr. Cromwell that some medication – Lithium specifically – was the same substance used in cellular phone batteries! To make my final point, I asked: "Can you imagine, right now, taking the back off your cell phone, chopping up the battery with a knife and swallowing it?! And you think *I* am crazy!!"

Disregarding my logic, the doctor explained that, due to my highly elevated mental state, I was jumping to conclusions. He went on to say that he did not intend for me to take Lithium in the first place. Instead, he suggested a more recently discovered, safer medication. But I knew as well as he did that "newer" and "safer" was medical code language for: This patient is "smarter" and "more educated" than I thought. And unfortunately for him, I already knew that even the "newer, better" medications still had numerous side-effects. "Now why," I thought to myself, "when I have made a point of avoiding alcohol and drugs for my entire life, would I now want to take drugs and blow a hole in my liver or fry my brain, or both?!"

As I continued to mentally formulate my next logical argument, I observed the look on the faces of both the social worker and the psych nurse that were observing my meeting. They silently seemed to scream, "There's no use – not if you ever want to get out of here!" In the moments that followed, it dawned on me. I realized that regardless of how logical my explanations were, or how vehemently opposed I was to taking medication, it really didn't matter. I was going to lose the game – no matter what. Confirming the conclusion I had just come to, Dr. Cromwell spoke calmly. Agreeing that he legally could not *force* me to take medication, he nobly granted me my freedom of choice. But in the same breath, he politely explained that I wouldn't be leaving the hospital until I *chose* to take it!! And with that, he stood up, smiled, shook my hand, and left the room.

What a jerk!

Back on the bed in my communal room, I laid down to think about what to do next. More than anything else I just wanted to get out of the hospital - and get out fast! Not only was the dark, dingy, depressing atmosphere so thick you could cut it with a knife, I didn't want to miss the birth of our third child. It was just too important, too special, too sacred. Closing my eyes as if to try and find the answer to my problem in some secret message scrawled on the inside of my eyelids, I decided the only way to get what I wanted was to obediently follow the doctor's orders − or at least make it *look* that way.

CHAPTER 23

The Plan

DING, DING, DING!!! Like a bell going off in my head it finally came to me! It was the perfect "technique", shall we say - the same one my friend Bob had used when *he* was locked up in a mental institution. Not really listening several years ago when he had told me about it, my subconscious mind must have recorded his words for possible future use. Thinking about the high level of difficulty in pulling off my deception, I reasoned that although it would not be easy, I was confident and smart enough to do it. And I was good-looking to boot, which would give me an advantage with the female nurses!

7:30 a.m.

Up early to shower and run through the plan in my mind.

7:40 a.m.

Dressed in casual, non-attention getting clothing, so as not to attract attention.

7:45 a.m.

Only 15 minutes until the loudspeaker call for medication.

7:46 a.m.

If Bob could do it, I can do it. I know God is on my side.

7:55 a.m.

Only five more minutes. Get ready to pour on the charm to distract the med nurse.

8:00 a.m.

Oh, Darn! I thought Kristy was the med nurse today, not John!!

8:02 a.m.

"Yes, John, it is surprising that, all of a sudden, I've decided to take my medication. You see, when I really thought about it, the doctor was right! And, as a matter of fact, so were you. I need these meds. Without them what kind of life would I have?" *(I can tell I'm flattering his ego.)*

8:03 a.m.

"Thanks for the pills, John. I guess this is just what I need to return to my normal state of mind."

8:04 a.m.

Man, these pills taste gross under my tongue!! Thank goodness John had his back turned and didn't notice that I didn't really swallow them.

8:05 a.m. (in the bathroom)

Pfffwww. Plink. Splash. I hope the red dye under my tongue isn't matched up with the red pills in the toilet.

8:06 a.m.

I did it!! Bob sure is sure a smart guy!

CHAPTER 24

Found Out!

7:30 a.m.

(Groggy thoughts): When I have no children to get off to school, no job to go to, no wife to nag me and no responsibilities, why on earth are they telling me I "have to" get up?

7:40 a.m.

Oh…darn! Oh…darn! Oh, darn! I guess they hadn't invented blood tests yet when Bob was in the Nut Hut. After they check my blood they will know what I've done!!!

I remember a funny story my Mom likes to tell every once in awhile. It seems that when I was a young child, I once took off my poopy diaper and, with my finger as a "brush," I began displaying my talent for art with smellier than usual brown paint, on the brilliant white, wall-sized "canvas" conveniently located in my bedroom. While I don't remember exactly what my mother said when she walked into the room, nor do I remember exactly how I felt about being caught… "brown-handed," when my name came over the loudspeaker directing me to meet with Dr. Cromwell "immediately!" I was pretty sure I was about to remember.

10:20 a.m.

So, that's how I must have felt when my mother discovered my prized painting. Well, at least with his accent, I couldn't really make out exactly what he was saying. It kinda sounded like he was not letting me go until something froze over, but with that thick, German accent, I could only guess what he was referring to.

• • •

Some people believe that getting what you want in life comes down to just "playing the game." But what are you supposed to do when the game isn't fair, and the odds are stacked so far against you it appears there is no hope of winning?! I concluded that all you can really do is fight back in whatever way you can. And fight back I would!!

Unbeknownst to my legend-in-his-own-mind doctor, I was just a tad smarter than most of his drug-laden, submissive patients. Through reading an article in a medical magazine I had found in the hospital, I realized that Dr. Cromwell had formed his conclusion about me spitting out my medication, partially based on assumption. How could I be so sure? The article highlighted the fact that only *one* of the two pills I had pretended to take could be detected in the blood.

So, true to my incredibly wise nature, I again began *actually* taking the one, while *continuing* to spit out the other. In so doing, I continued to fool the doctors and the nurses — even the really smart ones — day after day after day. Until one day, about a week later, something very strange and unexpected happened.

• • •

Note: The rest of Part 1: My True Story, is an explanation of my thoughts and feelings after "coming down" from my manic high, and returning to a more normal state of mind.

• • •

CHAPTER 25

Losing the High

During high school I found it interesting but sad to watch the cycle that many of my peers seemed to be stuck in: Go to school Monday to Friday, get drunk Friday and Saturday night, sober up all day Sunday, and go to school again on Monday. For many, this cycle seemed to serve their needs for pleasure and excitement really well for their teen years. For others, however, it seemed that being stuck in this destructive cycle also included doing things on the weekend that they would inevitably regret the morning after.

Though I did not participate, I observed the shame and embarrassment that resulted from these wild weekends, and the issues that had to be dealt with on the first day back to school. From little things like the guy apologizing to his girlfriend for hitting on another girl, to life changing events like when a bright, good-looking girl so starved for male attention would risk disease and/or pregnancy to get it.

Although I chose not to involve myself in this familiar teenage cycle, somehow, in some way, I was stuck in a very similar cycle. My cycle also involved deep regret, shame, and sorrow – somewhat similar to what those teenagers I knew may have felt.

While I felt many of the same feelings, however, the *source* of my shame and sorrow was quite different. You see, while growing up I observed many people who would say or do things I knew were not "normal". Even as a very young child, I knew this type of behavior was a direct result of a Mental Illness and I vowed *I* would never become like them.

But now I realized that I was exactly like them, and I was completely devastated!

I recalled that just over a year before I had had great aspirations of becoming very wealthy very quickly. I worked like a dog as a website advertising salesperson and was soon appointed "Director of Sales" of the new company. But all my hopes and dreams of becoming an overnight multi-millionaire were shattered when, just like now, everyone turned against me! They mistook my hard work, positive attitude and fearless dreaming for a serious mental problem. The result? Hospitalization - against my will.

Upon getting out of the hospital previously, I had felt more discouraged – not depressed – than I ever had up to that point in my life. At that time I determined that my low mood was *not* a problem with manic-depression, as the incompetent doctor thought. It was simply a result of stress overload.

Fortunately, after my first hospitalization, it only took me a few months to pick myself back up, find a new job, and begin again to work toward my goal of becoming an overnight millionaire.

But this time, while it was comforting to know that I didn't really spend hours gambling, with my head on the shoulder of *The* Jessica Simpson, it was also devastating to realize what a complete and utter fool I had been! More importantly, by leaving my responsibilities as a husband and father and escaping to Utah and then Nevada, I had broken the bond of trust I had established with Aimee and our children.

CHAPTER 26

Down & Out – Leaving the Hospital

Hearing my name over the loudspeaker announcing I had a visitor, was the moment I had been waiting for the entire three weeks I had been in hospital. While Aimee had visited me faithfully nearly every day, this day was different. Today I was actually going home.

As I grabbed my backpack and began heading down the dimly lit hallway toward the exit, I had very mixed emotions. On one hand I was over the moon that I was getting out of "jail", but on the other, I was scared to death at the prospect of facing *real* life and all the stress and challenges I blamed for putting me in the hospital in the first place.

After greeting Aimee with a hug and saying goodbye to a few nurses, we hopped in the elevator. When we reached the main floor I headed straight for the exit, as thoughts about my stay at the hospital flooded my mind. As we got in the car and started the 35 minute drive home, neither of us said much. It was definitely a moment of "awkward silence."

As we drove, deep feelings of regret and shame washed over me. I felt so disappointed in myself, so down, and so aware of Aimee's disappointment with me. Even though Aimee eventually started a conversation and pretended to be happy, I could tell she was uneasy around me. I really didn't blame her. Like me, she knew that while I was well enough to be released from the hospital, I was still in a very fragile state of mind.

In that state, we both knew, my moods and behaviors could be very unpredictable.

Even as Aimee talked, daunting questions flooded my mind. Would I continue to stay "down" for a few months like the last time, unable to get out of bed or look for a job? If I remained depressed and unable to look for work, how would we afford food and rent? If, by some miracle, I did land a job, would I be able to keep it for more than four months – a feat I had not yet accomplished in our seven-year marriage.

Next, my thoughts turned to our children. Would my head be clear enough to take part in the miracle of the birth of our third child? Was I capable of maintaining patience and understanding with our two young boys? Would the stress and lack of sleep that is a normal part of caring for a new baby send me into an even deeper depression? Or worse, would I react by going "high" again, ending up in Nevada all over again searching for some famous woman I felt destined to marry?

By the time we arrived home I had decided that, despite my best intentions, I was simply *not* capable of going out and looking for work. I was too down, too out, and too ashamed of where I had been. I didn't even feel capable of considering looking for work. While I knew my decision would not go over well with Aimee, I hoped she would understand that there was nothing I could do. Whether or not I actually had manic depression, or bi-polar disorder, I knew that trying to support a family when my mental state was so fragile was simply impossible. I was just not capable.

CHAPTER 27

Going from Bad to Worse

After the wonderful experience of seeing our first daughter born, my life seemed to go downhill. For the next three months I felt as if I was hopelessly stuck at the bottom of a deep, dark hole - a feeling that seemed to release it's firm grasp on me only when I was sleeping. My normally positive outlook on life was gone. I became absorbed in whatever it was that was wrong with me. Constant thoughts of all the responsibilities I was neglecting plagued my mind.

At that time, I was still pretty sure I was not really Mentally Ill. As much as I wanted to deny it, however, everything in my life – and everyone – seemed to point to that conclusion. The problem was, to me, admitting I had a Mental Illness would be like admitting I was the biggest, most hopeless waste of skin to ever walk the face of the earth. Doing so, I thought, would only lead to shunning and hating myself for the rest of my life. In short, if I *really* had a Mental Illness, I felt as if my life would be over. There would be no hope. *Nothing* would matter.

How could I be so sure? I knew how Mentally Ill people were perceived and treated. I knew how weak and emotionally unstable they were. In every case I was familiar with, Mental Illness meant a life-long struggle - a constant uphill battle - just to maintain a mental and emotional life that was somewhere near normal.

Questioning my sanity on a daily basis and hating myself more with each passing hour, I slowly and painfully endured, minute by minute, through the darkest, coldest, most sorrowful feelings I have ever felt. Through it all, while I recognized I had some kind of problem, I *refused* to admit to myself that I, of all people, was suffering from a Mental Illness.

My days were virtually all the same: Get out of bed around noon or 2 o'clock. Deal with the burden of guilt and shame for not going out and looking for a job. Next: Worry about how to keep our financial heads above water and pay off the $4,000 debt I had recklessly incurred on my manic "vacation" to Nevada.

Next, feeling as if I had weights tied to every part of my body, I would drag myself out of bed and into the bathroom. There, I would look at myself in the mirror with disgust and hate, and wish that I could live someone else's life, or at least stop living mine. Most days I craved the feeling of the hot water from the shower on my freezing body. Then it would take all my energy to get out of the shower and deal with the cool air against my skin. As I would wrap myself in a towel, I would curse the fact that I would have to dry off and then get dressed – an activity that usually took me well over an hour.

Sometimes in the mid-afternoon, finally dressed for the day, I would come out and give Aimee a big hug. I no longer hated her, nor did I want a divorce. In fact, I realized that without her to feed and take care of me, I could, quite possibly, die. I was just not capable of taking care of myself. Most times our hugs would include tears, sometimes from Aimee and sometimes from me – at least on those occasions when I was feeling "up" enough to cry. Then I would apologize to her for another day of not looking for work and for all the damage I had done and was continuing to do to our marriage and financial situation.

Throughout the day, our new baby girl would scream, cry, poop, pee, and spit-up like a normal baby should. But as much as I loved our daughter, I felt as if I just couldn't handle holding her for more than a few minutes – especially if she was crying. I blamed my deep feelings of depression for not even being able to enjoy this simple, beautiful pleasure.

Then one day, although I had tried to put the almost constant thought out of my mind for months, I decided that taking my own life would be the most appropriate way to deal with the overwhelming shame and hopelessness I felt. After all, how could someone officially diagnosed with a Mental Illness and who had spent time in *three* mental institutions in *two* different countries ever make it in the world? I still remember clearly the day, when I realized it was now or never.

CHAPTER 28

Suicide: The Logical Solution

M y wife, our two young children, and our new baby girl were at a birthday party. I knew I could leave a "letter of explanation" on the front door, which only *she* would be able to read. The children would never see my dead body and in the long run, they wouldn't even remember me. Not only would my wife be relieved of me – the biggest burden of her entire life – but she would finally be provided for financially by a life insurance policy that I knew included suicide.

But as I pictured it in my mind's eye – actually walking downstairs, loading my gun, putting it to my head and pulling the trigger – *something* or *someone* stopped me. From deep within my soul I felt a faint ray of hope, a feeling that I *was* worth something and that my life *was* worth living. Instead of taking action by taking my own life, I decided once and for all that the only type of action I would take from then on was the action of getting the help I so desperately needed.

Instead of being worried that I would be bothering my wife, or that her friends at the birthday party would think I was some kind of crazy, unemployed nut, I called her up and begged her to come home. When she finally arrived, I cried like a baby as I poured my heart out to her.

It was in that moment I realized for the first time that major, immediate, sweeping life change was no longer a matter of preference for me. *It had become a matter of life and death.* And as much as I wanted to continue to blame my childhood, my marriage, my parents, my failed businesses and all the people around me for the bottomless emotional pit that now held me captive, doing so would only be *continuing* the lie I had been telling myself for years. It would be feeding the very thing that had brought me to this point in my life. It would only perpetuate the deadly cycle that I was just beginning to realize I was in.

The fact was - I had finally hit *absolute rock bottom.* And although I was dazed and confused and in *excruciating* emotional pain, I was still around to talk about it. Somehow, through a literal miracle, I had resisted my terrible temptation.

God-willing, I knew that it was time to start crawling back up out of the deep, dark pit I was in. And, while I was full of intense fear and overwhelming anxiety, I also knew that somehow, someday - against all odds - I would eventually reach the top, crawl out, and declare victory.

PART 2
GETTING SERIOUS ABOUT CHANGE

CHAPTER 1

You Won't Fix What You Don't Know is Broken

In Part 1 you learned that I *almost* decided to take my own life before admitting I had a big problem with a Mental Illness.

While it's true that waiting so long to get help was harmful, I didn't do it intentionally. In fact, if I had truly understood that my years of denial would one day jeopardize my life, I never would have allowed myself to get to that point in the first place!

With that in mind, what we will discuss next is aimed at helping you decide for yourself (or someone you love) if *you* are in denial. If you are, Part 2 will attempt to convince you to get help *now*.

And while admitting you have a problem and getting help won't be easy in the short run, it may actually *save your life* in the long run.

MY STORY

A few years ago, shortly before my 2nd hospitalization, I found myself standing in a hot, soothing shower, reading a letter from my wife, Aimee. As if it wasn't bad enough that she was a terrible, insensitive wife, I wondered why she had now chosen to really come down hard on me.

As the soothing, hot water flowed over my body, I began to read her silly note. Beginning with a tactful mention of her concern for my mental state, she began by pleading with me to realize that I was beginning to get very "high." She also mentioned, point blank, that she knew I was dangerously close to needing to be hospitalized again. She further explained that although she had tried to reason with me and point out behaviours and attitudes that supported her belief, it seemed as if I would not listen.

Having full confidence in myself, however, and firmly believing Aimee was the one with the problem, I was disgusted that my own wife would try to control my life with threats of going to back to the hospital. Obviously, I was convinced, the letter and her concerns were nothing more than a futile attempt to get me to do what she wanted. And, when it came to the behaviours and attitudes she mentioned, such as extreme irritability, I knew that it was *her* fault. My irritable behaviour was simply a reaction to her need to control. On top of that, I rationalized, the stress I felt from our poor financial state would turn even the most mentally stable, positive person into a negative, angry cynic.

Next, she mentioned that I hadn't been getting enough sleep. "Yea, right," I thought as I shook my head in disgust. "Who is she to dictate to me – a grown man – how much sleep to get?" She then went on to remind me that my first hospital visit was due, in part, to ongoing sleep deprivation.

As if all her paranoia about irritability and lack of sleep wasn't bad enough, she had to bring in my eating habits, too. She *said* that it seemed that I never ate regular meals any more, and when I did, I didn't eat enough. This time I rolled my eyes in disgust. "Who is she – my mother?!" I thought to myself. "Why won't she just understand that I am too busy with work to eat regular meals? All I am trying to do is provide well for her and our children."

Finally, her letter outlined what she thought was my lack of ability to focus. From her perspective, she *thought* that I was taking on too much at work and at home. It also seemed to her that while my workload was heavy, my actual level of accomplishment was almost non-existent. Again, I rolled my eyes, wondering why I had been cursed with a wife who was only able to focus on the negative. "What a nag!" I thought to myself.

As I hopped out of the shower and put on my towel, I decided that it was time to set Aimee straight. I was really sick of her lack of support and bad attitude toward me. She never complimented me when I made a big sale at work, nor did she make any attempt to show me the love that I needed. All she did was criticize, nag, and complain. It was definitely high time to show her who was boss. If she didn't like what I had to say, that was fine. Nobody was forcing her to stay married to me. On the contrary, I could easily think of several reasons why divorce would be the best thing that ever happened to both of us.

PERCEPTION VS. REALITY

From where I am now in my life, reflecting on how I was thinking and what I was feeling while I read Aimee's letter, I feel pretty embarrassed. I now realize that Aimee was not against me at all, and that my problems would have only gotten worse if we had decided on divorce. In reality, the real problem was *me* and my altered perception of what was really going on.

Looking out of the window of my current state of Mental Wellness, I now see the truth in every single statement Aimee made in that letter. I can also see that, contrary to what I was convinced of at the time, Aimee was making a last ditch effort – out of love – to try and help me to see what was so obvious to her and everyone around me: My mental state was becoming increasingly fragile. My mood was very elevated – almost to the point of mania. Nobody could reason with me. She knew how much I hated going to the hospital and she desperately wanted to honor my wish of never returning. But she also knew that if I didn't "come back down" real fast, hospitalizing me would be her only option. Choosing to ignore her advice, Aimee's predictions materialized within a matter of a few short weeks.

A MESSAGE TO YOU

If you can relate – even in the slightest way – to how I felt as I read Aimee's letter, I have an important message for you: Now is the time – right now – to suck it up, bite your tongue, swallow your pride, get off your high horse, stop wallowing in your misery, forget about your self-pity, stop lying to yourself, and start listening to what your loved ones are saying.

BUT...THEY *ARE* OUT TO GET ME!

I really don't believe your loved ones are out to get you. *They* have not suddenly turned against you. *They* have not suddenly become irritable and angry and out of control. Like my line of thinking – that Aimee was off *her* rocker – consider the possibility that it is actually *you* who has the problem.

If your state of mind is currently what mine was when I read Aimee's letter, I expect that even the suggestion that *you* are the one with the problem is highly offensive to you. That's okay. I am not trying to tell you how to feel. I am simply asking you to *consider the possibility* that your perception is off. If it is, I hope you will consider the risks of continuing to live in your own, angry world.

CHAPTER 2

The Danger of Denial

MY WIFE'S FRIEND'S STORY

A few months ago we got a very disturbing phone call from one of Aimee's close friend's, Erin. It was about her sister Susan, who had come to visit with her two children, from New York. Apparently she was acting a little weird. Knowing she had a history of short manic episodes we decided to respond to Erin's request to come over and provide emotional support.

Susan, who was also a friend of ours from our school days, was a recently divorced, 30-year-old single Mom. According to Erin, Susan had planned the murder of her X-husband, John, whom we all knew she hated. If everything went according to Susan's plan, John would be dead within 12 hours!

While Susan's murder plans shocked Erin, she became gravely concerned about Susan's state of mind. Apparently, before coming to visit, she had explained to Erin that she had had little sleep and only enough food to sustain life. When Erin questioned why, Susan explained that she enjoyed the feeling it gave her.

As Aimee hung up the phone with Erin and began describing the situation to me, we both agreed that Susan was in desperate need of mental help!

STOPPING A MURDER

As you are well aware, horrific, terrible tragedies, such as murders, *do* happen as a direct result of Mental Illness. However, while we were worried for what was very clearly a manic psychosis, in Susan's case, we were definitely not worried for John's life. The reason was, in her state of mind, Susan did not comprehend that John was on a business trip thousands of miles away. Sadly, she was so far gone that she wouldn't have even been able to find John's location on a map, much less figure out how to get there and murder him that night.

As Aimee and I sped out to be with Erin before Susan harmed herself or someone else, we agreed that she would likely need to go to the hospital. Problem was, if she did, it could be the last nail in the coffin of John and Susan's ongoing custody battle, and would be just the evidence John needed to make his case in court for his X-wife's mental instability. If he could prove she actually had a Mental Illness, she could lose both kids for good.

EMPATHIZING WITH SUSAN

Now I don't know about you, but seeing Susan in a manic psychosis was truly one of the most interesting and scary things I have ever experienced. Watching her go through what I went through is something I will always remember.

After finally arriving, Aimee and I hopped out of the van and headed into the house. As we all began casually chatting and trying to explain to Susan why we were there, we wondered if Erin had made a mistake.

Susan actually appeared quite normal. In medical terms, she "presented well."

While we continued to engage her in conversation, Susan continued acting fairly normal. But before too long, her constant, eerie grin began to reveal what was really going on in her mind. Then, after about 10 minutes, she completely spilled the beans. When we questioned her as to why every light in the house was on (it was very sunny outside) she said that it was a necessary part of keeping "them" away. While Susan can be a joker at times, we realized that this time she was serious. As she continued her explanation, we discovered that "them" meant evil spirits, which she believed were trying to exert influence over her. Also noticing a difficult to describe dark and eerie feeling in the room, I wondered if, on this particular issue at least, maybe she was right.

A few minutes later, Susan opened up about her plans to kill John. She seemed to be somewhat unsure of her plan, however, and kept looking to Erin for reassurance. She also questioned us as to whether we had more information, as if she was in some kind of a bizarre, real-life murder mystery.

BETWEEN A ROCK AND A HARD PLACE

Emotionally drained from dealing with Susan, we all breathed a sigh of relief when, after two intense hours, she finally went to sleep – at least for a few minutes. While she slept, Erin and Aimee and I discussed the pros and cons of hospitalization.

Besides the fact that she did not have medical insurance, we were most concerned about how her hospitalization would affect her custody rights. On top of all that, we also discussed the question of whether we had the right to make such a potentially life-altering decision on Susan's behalf.

After making a few phone calls to several local hospitals and mental health facilities, we decided to take the advice given to us. The most important thing, we were assured, was Susan's safety - as well as our own.

In the end, we ended up taking Susan to the hospital. Uncontrollable and completely unwilling to stay, the nurses, doctors and security workers became convinced that she was, in fact, a potential danger to herself or others and escorted her to the psych ward. Diagnosed as having manic-depressive illness, or bi-polar disorder as it is also known, she was held in hospital for a week.

CHAPTER 3

Scenario # 1 or Scenario # 2?
The Choice is Yours

HOSPITAL AFTERMATH

Knowing that putting her in the hospital would not go over well, Erin was just a little bit concerned when Susan was discharged later that week. She called and asked us to come over again when she arrived home from the hospital.

Surprisingly, the moment Susan walked in the door she singled out Erin and began an intense verbal assault. "How could you make the decision to put me into the hospital!? Don't you realize if John finds out about this I will lose my kids!? Why couldn't you see I just needed more sleep!? Were you just too stupid to see that I was just on stress overload!? Do you realize that because of you I may never have custody of my children again!? What makes you think YOU had the right to put me in a mental hospital!? You had no right, Erin! You had no right!!"

Having been prepared for an attack, Erin's response was calm but firm. She explained: "I know you are angry right now, Susan, but what we did was motivated by love and concern for you and your safety, and the safety of your children. In fact, at one point, you even *agreed with us* about your need to be hospitalized."

Thinking that Susan may have understood her sister's logic, I was a taken aback as she began her next verbal assault. As Erin clenched her teeth and shook her head we all realized it was hopeless – at least for now. Susan was in a state of complete and utter denial. Bottom line: In her disturbed, self-centered state, the facts didn't really matter, and no amount of calm, logical explanation was going to change her mind.

INSANITY

They say the definition of insanity is this: Doing the same things over and over again but expecting different results. In Susan's case, and earlier in my own life, I was sure that everything and everyone else on earth was to blame for what was happening to me. I rationalized that I was stressed. I was out of work. My mother did a poor job of raising me. My father didn't show me enough love. My wife didn't love me any more. In short, I was absolutely convinced that everyone else was to blame for my problems, and that I was NOT responsible for my mental state. Instead, I was sure that I was a victim – a victim of circumstance, a victim of stress, and a victim of people who hated me and were mean and cruel.

VICTIM MODE

Having overcome my Mental Illness, I now understand that *regardless of all the excuses a person may have for being in "Victim Mode," remaining in this state doesn't do a darn thing to help you get out of it!* And whether it is Susan, or me, or you, or anyone who continues to live in Victim Mode, that person will continue to live in an emotionally unstable, angry and irritable world – a world *they* have created for *themselves*.

So how does all this relate to you? What can you do if you are stuck in Victim Mode? The answer is simple: It is time for you to go out on a limb and make one of the most important decisions of your entire life – a decision that will be life-altering and have far reaching consequences. This is where push comes to shove, where you fish or cut bait, you're either in or out.

SCENARIO # 1

At this moment you have an opportunity - a huge opportunity - to solve some of your biggest problems and get on with the business of living a happy, successful life. Despite what you may think at this moment, you *can* overcome whatever mental and emotional challenges you have. I know, because I have been there and I have done it.

I speak from experience when I say you *can* turn you life around. You *can* create for yourself, a life of happiness and success, regardless of how hopeless that goal may seem at this moment, or how many times you have failed in the past.

If you decide to make a go of it, you are in for a lot of hard work and some real life changes that you have likely never experienced before – some that you may see as absolutely beyond your reach or even impossible. But don't worry. If all this talk about change is beginning to sound a little scary, don't despair. There is another solution. What I have described here is only Scenario # 1. In Scenario # 2, things are much easier.

SCENARIO # 2

If you choose Scenario # 2 you will, for a while, be really happy in comparison to the first scenario I have described. You see, in Scenario #

2, you get to be like Susan. You get to continue your angry, emotional outbursts. You still get to ignore the poor state of your Mental Health and all the problems you create for yourself as a result of your denial. But wait, that's not all! The best part of living (or continuing to live) a "Scenario # 2" lifestyle, is - and this is a doozy - it is *not your fault!* You get to blame everyone else, including your mother, your father, your husband, your wife, your children, your boss, or anyone else you can think of – beginning with your childhood right on up to the present. Heck, you can even blame people you may meet in the future! In fact, you can blame whomever or whatever your bitter, angry mind can come up with, and you don't even have to feel bad about it! You see, in Scenario # 2, there's simply nothing you can do about it. That's just the way you are.

As you may have guessed, Scenario # 2 also allows you to continue believing that you are a victim. The great part about that is that *it requires no further effort on your part.* There is no work, no sacrifice, no responsibility.

If you are pretty sure you have a mental and/or emotional problem, but are quite adamant that *everyone else* in the universe is responsible for it, I would suggest that you are settling for Scenario # 2.

REALITY CHECK

If you think that the success and happiness in life you deserve has been robbed from you by other people or circumstances beyond your control, I've got news for you: it ain't! And until you decide to choose Scenario # 1 over Scenario # 2, you will continue to live in a world filled with feelings of bitterness, constant anger, intense self-pity and harsh injustice.

Take it from someone who has been there.

Alternatively, however, you can make a better choice. You can suck it up, make a firm decision to change, work like you've never worked before, focus on actually overcoming your Mental Illness, follow your dreams, and ultimately create for *yourself* a life full of constant happiness, intense joy, and deep inner peace.

Now I'm not one to impose on your sense of right or wrong, or to infringe on your God-given right to choose, but if you want my opinion, it's a heck of a lot easier and a lot more fun *in the long run*, to invest in yourself - today. You see, the time and effort required to make the sacrifices in Scenario # 1 now, far outweigh the so-called benefits of remaining in a state of denial, anger, and mental and emotional instability that characterizes Scenario # 2.

CHAPTER 4

The Power of Admitting You Have a Problem

SO, NOW WHAT DO I DO?

According to the U.S. Department of Health and Human Services, a Mental Illness "changes the way that (a) person thinks, feels, and/or behaves. Mental disorders lead to distress and/or impaired functioning and produce a host of problems that may include disability, pain, and even death."

Hundreds of different forms of "Mental Disorders" or Mental Illnesses have been identified by the medical community. These include: depression, manic depression (also known as bi-polar disorder), schizophrenia, anxiety disorders, eating disorders, and post partum depression, to name just a few.

Of course, nearly all Mental Health organizations agree that with help, people can learn to cope with, and even recover from a Mental Illness.

GETTING HELP

Perhaps the most difficult challenge I have ever faced in dealing with my Mental Illness was the all-important step of getting help. Denial was, in many ways, a much easier route than actually admitting I had a problem and taking responsibility. It was much easier on my ego too. You see, as I explained earlier, if I *actually* had a mental problem, I believed that my life as I knew it would be over. My whole world would be shattered. My perception of who I was and what I was about would be forever scarred. I would no longer be capable of seeing myself as a strong, self-confident, good-looking man, but would feel like a weak, insecure, mentally unstable idiot, who was blessed to at least still have his good looks. ☺

Fortunately, in the long run, my decision to get help by ignoring my ego and putting to rest my false beliefs about Mental Illness was the best thing that ever happened to me. Later, I will go into detail about the positive after-affects I experienced as a result of this decision. But for now, just trust that what I am saying is true.

Below is a short list of typical adult signs and/or symptoms that may indicate the presence of a Mental Disorder:

- Persistant sad, anxious, or "empty" mood
- Feelings of guilt, worthlessness, helplessness
- Anxiety
- Nervousness
- Extreme anger
- Inability to cope with normal life stresses
- Abuse of drugs/alcohol
- Extreme irritability
- Increased negativity

- Changes in appetite
- Not keeping appointments
- Displaying of irrational thought patterns
- Poor judgement
- Lack of concentration
- Lack of motivation
- Being obsessed with something that doesn't really matter
- Thoughts of suicide
- Spending Sprees

If you, or someone you love is experiencing any of these symptoms and are at a loss for what to do, I sincerely hope that you will continue to read this book. If you do, it is my firm conviction that what you read will help you in ways you may have never thought possible.

EVEN IF I WANT TO CHANGE, I DON'T KNOW IF I CAN

Started in 1935 by two American men, a stockbroker and a surgeon who were both "hopeless drunks," Alcoholics Anonymous has helped millions of people throughout the world overcome their alcoholism (classified as a form of Mental Illness) and regain control of their lives. Through a now famous "12 Step Program", almost anyone addicted to alcohol can get the help and support they need from people who know, from personal experience, what they are going through. And, according to their website, www.alcoholics-anonymous.org, the only requirement for membership is a desire to stop drinking.

As one who has been there - not with alcoholism, but with mania and depression - I have an important message for you: If you will do nothing more at this moment than reach within your soul and grasp onto *a desire* to change, I promise you that you will instantly become empowered to begin your journey down the road that leads to success in overcoming your Mental Illness.

CHAPTER 5

Life Lessons, by Martha Stewart

MY STORY

After being released from hospital the second time, I made yet another unwise decision that immediately began to negatively affect the state of my Mental Health. It was a decision motivated by a desire for two "rights" that I had not yet matured enough to earn – freedom and independence. My decision: to stop taking my medication.

At that point in my life, I was able to justify my actions and rationalize my decision based on what I felt were solid, logical reasons. On top of that, I "knew" that all the doctors and nurses, who had strongly advised me to keep taking my medication after being released from hospital, were wrong. What they did not know was that *I* was different. *I* could take care of myself, and no person or pill would ever change that. *I* was just too strong.

A CHANGE OF HEART

However, a few weeks later, as we were driving home from visiting the in-laws, I began to have a change of heart. It all happened during a casual conversation with Aimee when I realized I was becoming extremely defensive and angry. I could tell that I was really over-reacting, but it was as if I couldn't control what I was saying. But then something really weird happened.

While I don't recall exactly what either of us said, I remember the feeling I had as clearly as if it were yesterday. For just a few minutes, I was given the gift of insight into how I would look to someone else – someone who was calm, genuinely self-confident, and mentally and emotionally grounded. And in my mind's eye, I began to see myself as if I were a different person.

In so doing, I recognized that this angry man (me) was blowing everything Aimee said completely out of proportion. As the conversation continued, it didn't matter what his (my) wife said, or how kindly she said it, he was upset by every single word. Thinking at first this person was a complete jerk – any woman's worst nightmare – I began to feel sorry for this angry, irritable man. Somewhere, past the put downs and immature behaviour, was a kind and loving soul. And although the man was definitely out of control, I perceived that in a very desperate way, he didn't want to be. It was almost as if he didn't know how to feel or react any other way. In fact, at the deepest level, he desperately *wanted* to change. He *wanted* to control his anger. He *wanted* to cool his temper. He *wanted* to treat his wife and children so well that one day, he would have the privilege of hearing them call him their hero. Problem was, he just didn't know how.

With that insight, I returned back to my world of anger and resentment. Although I still felt emotionally out of control, I now realized that

I needed help in a bad way. I hated the way I was arguing with my wife. I hated losing my temper all the time. I hated putting her down all the time — especially in front of our impressionable young children.

For over seven years of marriage I had continued to live this way. But in that moment I realized that not only was I an emotional drain on Aimee, I was emotionally draining *myself*! I felt so tired, so worn out, so negative! I was sick of it. I had had enough. I was willing to do whatever it would take to change.

IT'S A "MARTHA-THING"

Like Martha Stewart finally deciding it was pointless to continue trying to prove her innocence and just get her jail time over with, I was ready to do whatever it took. As soon as we arrived home, I jumped out of the car and headed directly for the kitchen. I removed a chair from the table and slid it across the floor over to the fridge. I eagerly hopped on the chair, opened the cupboard, and began scrounging around. Finding my dreaded bottle of medication, given to me before leaving the hospital, I quickly read the label, opened the container and removed two small pink pills. Grabbing a glass of water and putting the pills in my mouth, I no longer felt the intense fear I had felt in the hospital. Instead, as I drowned my pills in water and sent them rushing down my throat, I felt an incredible sense of relief, a kind of peace I had never felt before.

NOWHERE TO GO BUT UP

The decision I made that day involved much more than just going on medication intended to level out my moods. That day I committed to myself to do *whatever it would take* to overcome my Mental Illness. Several years later, I am happy to report that my mission has been wildly successful. I no longer struggle with a Mental Illness, but instead, focus on a daily routine of doing those things that I know will continue to sustain my Mental Wellness.

• • •

The purpose of this book is to share with you the principles and techniques that I know - *from personal experience* - will work in your quest to successfully overcome your Mental Illness. Before we go any further, however, it will be helpful to review what we have just discussed in Part 2 – Getting Serious About Change.

1. Nothing will change unless you take responsibility for yourself and admit you have a problem. Doing so actually constitutes strength of character, not weakness, as I used to think.

2. You have the right to choose denial. In fact, if you choose, you can live in denial forever. However, while the choice is all yours, so are the consequences. Continuing to live in denial will only jeopardize the most important aspects of your life: your family relationships, your ability to become emotionally and mentally stable, and ultimately, your ability to create for yourself a life of happiness, inner peace and success.

3. Through using the list of signs and symptoms found at the beginning of Chapter 4, you can determine for yourself, or for a loved one, the probability that you (or they) have a Mental Illness. Even though realizing that you have a Mental Illness can lead to the deflation of your ego, it is well worth it.

4. Love her or hate her, Martha Stewart's buck-stops-here example of just going to jail while maintaining her innocence, also applies to you or your loved one. While getting help can be difficult and emo-

tionally painful in the short run, it is the quickest and best solution in the long run.

If you are serious about change - and I sincerely hope that you are - it is time to make your commitment official. On the next page is a document that will be a great help to you in accomplishing your goal of overcoming your Mental Illness.

This contract with yourself will help you to keep going when the going gets tough. Re-reading your contract on a regular basis will help you recall the feelings of conviction and determination you had at the time you signed it.

MY COMMITMENT TO LIFE-LONG
MENTAL WELLNESS & SUCCESS

By signing this contract, I, _____,
hereby commit to do *whatever it takes* to accomplish my goal
of becoming and remaining Mentally Well for the rest of
my life.

With the knowledge that I am a Child of God, and that He
believes in me and will help me, I resolve to always believe
in *myself* and my ability to accomplish my goal.

I understand that keeping my commitment will involve
hard work and self-discipline. I resolve to do the work and
to develop the discipline.

When the going gets tough, or if I ever feel like giving up,
I will re-read this contract and remind myself of my commitment to becoming and remaining Mentally Well for the
rest of my life, and to believing in my ability to do anything
I put my mind to.

Signed

_____

(Your Name Here)

Date:

PART 3

FROM STIGMA TO SUCCESS

———————

• • •

Your life *is* worth something. You *are* capable. You *can* do it.

Your life *is* worth living and it *doesn't* have to be full of pain and sorrow

The same God who put you here on earth never intended for you to fail.

He knows you are capable of great things.

His greatest desire is to see you succeed in all areas of your life.

• • •

CHAPTER 1

Turning Lemons into Lemonade

FROM SOUR TO SWEET

With your official Commitment to Life-Long Mental Wellness and Success in place, you are ready to take the next step. This step deals with the way you perceive your Mental Illness.

In *Part 3, From Stigma to Success,* you will learn how to turn your negative attitudes and beliefs about Mental Illness into something much more useful. In this part, I will show you how to turn your "lemons" into lemonade. The great thing is, although your sour experiences remain a part of unchangeable history, the lemonade you make from them can make your future the most exquisite, sweet – tasting drink you've ever had!

MY STORY

Having always prided myself on being strong-minded and independent, to me Mental Illness was something *other* people (emotionally unstable, weird people) had to deal with. Having held this perception since childhood, it is not hard to explain why, for a long time after my hospitalizations, I was plagued with heart-wrenching feelings of injustice and inner hate as well as self-pity, denial and depression, from which I was sure I would never recover.

Not being one to give up on a challenge, however, I decided the only way to overcome my so - called mental disorder was to face it head on.

Through extremely honest inner reflection and endless hours of soul - searching, I came to two conclusions:

1. As much as I hated to admit it, I did have a real problem with emotional and mental stability.

2. Despite my natural inclination to blame everyone and everything else in my life, I knew that taking personal responsibility was the only way I would ever recover.

Looking back, understanding those two facts made all the difference in helping me change my life to where I am now: a happily married, Mentally Well, proud father of four children who is passionate and determined to help *you* overcome *your* Mental Illness too.

HOW I CAN HELP YOU

Bottom Line: Unlike nearly all Mental Health experts who advise their Mentally Ill patients based on theoretical knowledge, *I have actually been there.* Unlike them, I have actually experienced - not just read about - many of the same feelings and thoughts that you may be having.

I know *firsthand* the feeling of hopelessness, depression and despair. *I know what it feels like* to feel so stressed and incapable of coping with life that you just want to run away and hide. I have *actually harboured self-hate* to the point that I wanted desperately to kill myself. I have *felt the torment* that accompanies these intense urges. *I have fought the battle* and I am still here to talk about it.

Finding happiness and success through overcoming my Mental Illness – a feat I was once convinced was impossible – is now a reality for me. I want it to be *your* reality too.

CHAPTER 2

Getting Rid of Your B.S.

MY STORY

Several months ago, I overheard a conversation between some of the neighbourhood children regarding our five-year-old son. As he was performing a daring and attention - getting stunt on our backyard fence, I heard one of the five-year-old girls say "Wow, Harrison, you are a psycho-boy. You're crazy, Harrison." Most of the other children nodded in agreement and added their comments, which were all along the same lines. Shaking my head in disbelief I left the yard and went back into the house.

A few days later as my wife and I and our four young children played in the park, I was reminded of what happened. While watching his young son do something daring on the swings, a young father remarked that his son was "crazy." As we were leaving, I heard him say something like: "Wow, Johnny, you better stop doing that or they will take you away to *Ponoka*" (the local, well - known mental institution).

Hearing that father's words brought back painful memories of the shame and self-hate I felt when I was actually institutionalized in "Ponoka." More importantly though, I realized that this young child,

along with my own young children and their friends, were already well
- educated in society's view of Mental Illness.

Whether it is society's way of explaining abnormal behaviour or an
attempt to deal with the fear that often surrounds it, the question of *why*
a Mental Illness carries with it a HUGE negative stigma is completely
irrelevant. It just doesn't matter. What does matter, however, is how you,
as a person with a Mental Illness, or as the loved one of someone who is
struggling with it, deals with it.

TO GET HELP OR NOT TO GET HELP, THAT IS THE QUESTION

Unfortunately, the vast majority of people choose to deal with the
Stigma by simply not dealing with it.

According to the National Institute of Mental Health (N.I.M.H.),
over 50 million Americans have a mental disorder in any given year.
Sadly, however, research by the N.I.M.H. and other mental health organizations reveals that while treatment for a Mental Illness is *almost always
successful*, less than 7.5 million people, or just under 15%, ever seek treatment in the first place!

CAN YOU REALLY BLAME THEM?

One of the top reasons identified for this unfortunate statistic (and
one that I can identify with strongly) is that a majority of people are
just plain embarrassed about the state of their emotional and Mental
Health.

Probably feeling like I used to, they believe that being labelled with
a Mental Illness is a lot like walking around in public with a large sign
around their necks that reads:

"Kick me - I'm an Idiot!"

GETTING RID OF YOUR B.S.

If you can relate to how I used to feel, it is high time to get rid of the B.S. that is causing you to think this way.

Getting rid of your B.S. – your **B**elief **S**ystem about Mental Illness can be accomplished in two easy steps:

1. Consider the possibility that your current Belief System about Mental Illness is flawed.

2. Form a new, accurate Belief System.

As I began to get rid of *my* B.S. and form a new Belief System, I realized that, contrary to everything I had always believed, struggling with a Mental Illness did not make me an idiot! On the contrary, I now understand that I was a wonderful, smart, handsome man with a problem. That problem, while very, very challenging, was not impossible to overcome.

As one who has had *personal experience*, I am here to tell you that you, too, can overcome your Mental Illness and eventually lead a normal, happy, successful life.

CHAPTER 3

Buying into the Stigma: Your Choice

I'M NOT ONE OF "THEM"

"Not me!" you may be saying to yourself right now. "I am a strong person. I don't need help!" "I am not "crazy," you may rationalize, "and I am definitely not going to visit a shrink!" (After all, what would the neighbours say if they found out?!)

Three years ago I would have been right there with you. Beginning in early childhood I became well - acquainted with the behaviours and attitudes exhibited by people struggling with a Mental Illness. These people were close relatives like the aunt who would fly off the handle and scream at her children for no reason. They were the "weirdo's" like the woman who stood up in the middle of church and started swearing a blue streak. They were the "schizo's" like the man who would wander the streets asking himself questions and then answering them. They were the "psycho's" like the police officer who hung himself after his wife left him.

But time and experience has an interesting way of changing the way you think, and I can now say with complete confidence that being institutionalized was the beginning of the best thing that ever happened to me.

ARE YOU NUTS??!!

As I began my quest to overcome my Mental Illness, the # 1 roadblock I was up against was Stigma. Later, I realized that my # 1 opponent in overcoming the Stigma of *my* Mental Illness was *me*! While that statement may sound "crazy," and while you may even think I am "nuts", keep reading to find out why I would say such a thing.

CHAPTER 4

Stigma: A Matter of Life and Death

MY STORY

After I got out of the hospital, buying into the Stigma about people struggling with a Mental Illness almost resulted in a decision to end my life. Thankfully however, I realized, Stigma or not, things were going to change in my life.

While my story is one of success, there are far too many that are not. According to the National Institute of Mental Health (N.I.M.H.), hundreds of thousands of Americans try to take their own lives each year. Tragically, over 30,000 are successful. As a result, *suicide is the 11ᵗʰ leading cause of death in the United States!*

If you find yourself among the tens of millions of people who need help but for whatever reason are not getting it, I have an important message for you: Now is the time – right now – to decide to change. I have felt many of the same feelings of embarrassment, shame, self-pity and hate, denial, and depression that you may be feeling.

I know what it's like to believe that killing yourself or continuing on in abnormal, dangerous behaviour can be a more attractive option than the "embarrassment" of getting help. I have felt the fear of being labelled as being "Mentally Ill" and I am here to tell you that confronting it is hard. Really hard.

But despite what society may think, and despite the unfair Stigma that accompanies Mental Illness, *you* can become successful in overcoming your problem if you are willing to put in the sweat and tears that this type of an undertaking requires.

So forget the Stigma! Forget what society has taught you! Stop worrying about what your friends and relatives or even your spouse will think of you! Instead, start believing that you are a person of Infinite Worth — a literal Child of God.

The truth is, your life *is* worth something. You *are* capable. You *can* do it. Your life *is* worth living and it *doesn't* have to be full of pain and sorrow. The same God who put you here on earth never intended for you to fail. *He* knows you are capable of great things. *His* greatest desire is to see *you* succeed in all areas of your life.

With all my heart I urge you to think deeply about the truth of what you have just read. I sincerely hope that you will decide to make the life changes your soul has been longing for.

You *are* worth it!!!

CHAPTER 5

Stigma: Advice from an Insider

GROUP # 1

When it comes to the struggle surrounding a Mental Illness, there are two main groups involved. The first group is made up of people like you and I – people who have been *personally* affected by it.

GROUP # 2

The second group are people who have not personally been affected by a Mental Illness, but have definitely been *indirectly* affected in some way. This group includes people like: my wonderful wife and many other spouses, the business owner with an alcoholic employee, the mother whose daughter struggles with an eating disorder, and/or an entire country horrified by a tragic train derailment caused by a suicidal man.

HELP FOR GROUP # 2

For whatever reason, there are loads of books out there to help people in Group # 2 cope with those of us in Group # 1. Many are written by medical professionals and/or relatives of those who have struggled with a Mental Illness. My research of this literature reveals that many of the authors are kind, compassionate people who genuinely want to help other people.

Problem is, when the majority of the literature is produced by people who only have second – hand information and experience, the ideas and techniques presented tend to be fairly one-sided. Now, don't get me wrong. Many of these books contain excellent information that can be very helpful to those of us in Group # 1. But there are also false beliefs that continue to be perpetuated by those who don't have a clue what it is like to *personally* struggle with a Mental Illness.

STIGMA

Dealing with the Stigma associated with a Mental Illness is front and centre when it comes to these false beliefs.

Regardless of what group you are in, the information presented in the next few chapters will help you understand why such a negative Stigma still exists. You will also learn what you can do about it.

But before you continue reading, STOP! It is time to put on your "I like change" hat. What you are about to read probably goes against everything you have ever learned or believed about Stigma.

So feel free to be skeptical. Feel free to disagree. All I ask is that you read to the end of *Part 3 – From Stigma to Success* and decide for yourself if what I'm saying is true. I also ask you to consider the *source* of the information you are about to read. As a person who has *personally* struggled with a Mental Illness, I have *first-hand* experience in dealing with Stigma.

STIGMA DEFINED

A quick search on Google reveals what the website of the U.S. Department of Health and Human Services★ has to say about Stigma as it relates to a Mental Illness. "Stigma is not just the use of the wrong word or action. Stigma is about disrespect. It is the use of negative labels to identify a person living with mental illness. Stigma is a barrier and discourages individuals and their families from getting the help they need due to the fear of being discriminated against."

In further searching on this website, people from Group # 1 and Group # 2 who need help will find a list of Do's and Don'ts when it comes to Stigma. Listed below are just three:

Don't use generic labels such as retarded, or the mentally ill.

Don't use terms like crazy, lunatic, manic depressive, or slow functioning.

Do use respectful language.

★Source: Substance Abuse and Mental Health Services Administration (SAMHSA) of the United States Department of Health and Human Services on their National Mental Health Information Center Website (www.mentalhealth.org)

If you are in Group # 2, this advice may appear to be sound, logical advice from an extremely credible source. However, as a Group # 1 member, those in Group # 2 need to know that advice like that, while intended to help, *is actually perpetuating the Stigma that surrounds Mental Illness. In short, it is doing more harm than good!!!*

So now that you really have your back up, read on. I believe you will yet become convinced.

CHAPTER 6

Jim Carrey, Wimps, and You

A BEAUTIFUL MIND

E ver seen the movie *A Beautiful Mind* with Russell Crowe and Jennifer Connelly? Ever wonder how a movie about the delusions of a Schizophrenic man who wins a Nobel Prize ended up becoming a blockbuster hit? Could it be that such a high level of achievement by someone with such a serious Mental Illness is so unheard of that everyone wanted to see it?

In all honesty, at the time *A Beautiful Mind* was a popular new movie, I wanted to see it for that very reason. But since then my attitude has changed and my understanding of why most of us never hear the "good news" stories about Mental Illness has expanded.

I now understand that there are many highly successful, famous people in this world who have struggled with a Mental Illness. Take Jim Carrey, for example, who has struggled with manic depression. Stories like his are more common than you might think. But why do we rarely hear them?

I believe there are two main reasons:

1. Unfortunately, as anyone in the media will admit, "good news" stories are not the main focus of the media. Instead, because of public

demand, the media tends to cater to what their audience wants. As a result, "bad news" stories are more commonly reported.

2. Many famous, wealthy people who have overcome a Mental Illness simply do not broadcast their story to the world. Can you really blame them? With the way society currently views someone with a Mental Illness, I certainly don't! Since we have already discussed Jim Carrey, lets use his story as a simple example.

JIM CARREY'S STORY

Jim Carrey, once a "no-name," struggling actor who is now undeniably successful in his field, admitted on television that he has struggled with a Mental Illness. I was a little surprised by his admission, but not surprised that he did not volunteer the information to his interviewer. Rather, he decided to be honest when asked. In my opinion, Jim Carrey's "success story" despite his struggle with a Mental Illness should have been all over the news the next day. Unfortunately it wasn't.

But what if he had tried to commit suicide, or attempted to murder his wife? I'm sure you would agree that nearly every media outlet in the country would have scrambled to be the first to report the story.

THE STORY OF VERY WELL-MEANING PEOPLE

While not in the mainstream of society, there is another group that we have not yet discussed. The people who make up this group, Group # 3, recognize that a mother who drowns her children, or a father who sets the house on fire with his children inside are not "psycho," but are struggling with an out-of-control Mental Illness. Motivated by genuine compassion, many well – meaning people in this group often make sincere attempts to help eradicate Stigma and foster understanding.

While I take my hat off to these people and their attempts to make the world a better place, many times their best efforts are misguided. Why? Due to a lack of *first*-hand experience many believe that the "Mentally Ill" of the world need someone – anyone – to protect and take care of them.

Why? I guess they believe that people struggling with a Mental Illness are incapable of protecting and taking care of *themselves*. So like a young child in the care of a parent, this "strong" group of people take charge. Motivated by what they think is love, they do everything in their power to ensure that nobody does or says anything that could hurt the tender feelings of their precious, helpless "child." But when it comes to protection, what kind of message are they really sending to the one being protected?

MY STORY

As a young child my loving father was very protective of me. From what I could tell, his noble desire to protect *me* was a direct result of the hurt *he* felt as a child when he was ridiculed for being skinny and non-muscular.

Consequently, I learned early in my life never to use the word, "wimp," because of the intense pain and suffering it could cause someone like me, a naturally skinny and non-muscular boy. Dad would also stick up for me and correct anyone that used the "W" word in his presence or tried to do anything that would potentially hurt my feelings.

But once I began school I realized I had a major problem. Without the protection of my father, I began to get picked on. Without Dad around other children began to tease me, and I became easily hurt by their put downs. Perhaps worst of all, the boys – and even some girls – had the gall to use the most hurtful of all words, and I was often referred to as a…"wimp."

When kids on the playground were mean to me I knew Dad would be absolutely furious. But since he was no longer around to protect me I was left to defend *myself*. I often felt ashamed and hurt and wondered why I had been cursed with my body type. Without Dad, I felt completely helpless. I became unsure of myself and my abilities, and longed for the comfort and protection I felt when Dad was around.

THE RESULT

When I became a father I vowed to be just like *my* loving father. I promised myself I would be vigilant in protecting my children and anyone else whom I believed needed protection. And up until a few years ago I believed this protection was important – even essential. After all, I thought, if *I* didn't protect my children and others who were incapable of protecting themselves, who would?!

CHAPTER 7

Protection Campaign

PROTECTION ON A HUGE SCALE

J ust like my father went to great lengths to protect me, many people from Group # 2, and Group # 3 also believe there is a need to protect people who are struggling with a Mental Illness.

But this line of thinking is fundamentally flawed because it is based completely on the assumption that those being protected are incapable of protecting *themselves*.

Not yet convinced?

The following campaign launched a few years ago in Britain by the Royal College of Psychiatrists, illustrates my point:

CAMPAIGN TO END STIGMA OF MENTAL ILLNESS*

Experts are launching a campaign aimed at reducing the stigma attached to mental illness.

The "Changing Minds: Every Family" campaign from the Royal College of Psychiatrists (RCP) is part of a five-year programme which hopes to change people's attitudes and behaviour towards the mentally ill.

The campaign follows recent controversy over the early release of a man who attacked churchgoers with a Samurai sword and the man who stabbed ex-Beatle George Harrison.

Posters featuring catchphrases such as "Can't talk to that nutter" above the slogan "Stop. Think, Understand." will appear on 2,000 London Underground tube train panels during the next month.

The "Changing Minds" campaign also wants to end stereotypical and stigmatising representations of the mentally ill in the media and elsewhere.

Words such as "nutter", "psycho" and "schizo" are derogatory and should not be used, they say.

A spokesman for the RCP said: "There should be no room for stigma in the third millennium.

"The Changing Minds campaign is trying, in a variety of ways, to encourage everyone to stop and think about their own attitudes and behaviour in relation to mental disorders."

"At the same time, we need to remind ourselves that, directly or indirectly, some form of mental health problem affects every family in the UK."

"The experience of our patients is that discriminatory attitudes are widespread within the general public, the medical profession, employers, banks, insurance companies and many other organisations."

Margery Wallace, chief executive of the charity SANE, said: "We hope that people will see the adverts on the Tube, and that the campaign will help mentally ill people themselves who so often feel sidelined and out of synch with society to feel that they belong and that someone is there to help."

The charity's helpline, Saneline, can be contacted on 0845 767 8000.

*Source: BBC News Website: www.news.bbc.co.uk

CAMPAIGN ANALYSIS

While the goal of the campaign was to "reduce the stigma attached to mental illness", in reality, campaigns like this actually *strengthen* the Stigma.

The following *new* campaign will help illustrate the truth of what I am saying.

CAMPAIGN TO END STIGMA OF OBESITY★

Experts are launching a campaign aimed at reducing the stigma attached to plus-size individuals.

The "Changing Minds: Every Family" campaign from the Royal College of Physicians & Surgeons (RCPS) is part of a five-year program which hopes to change people's attitudes and behaviour towards the body-mass challenged.

The campaign follows recent media reports about the significant weight gain of Kirstie Alley, the Emmy Award-Winning, so-called "Fat Actress" who starred in the hit T.V. series "Cheers".

Posters featuring catchphrases such as "Here Comes Large Marge!" above the slogan "Stop. Think, Understand." will appear on 2,000 Chicago subway train panels during the next month.

The "Changing Minds" campaign also wants to end stereotypical and stigmatizing representations of the body-mass challenged in the media and elsewhere.

Words and phrases such as "fatso," "tub of lard," and "fat chance" are derogatory and should not be used, they say.

A spokesman for the RCPS said: There is no room (no pun intended) for the stigma of plus-size individuals in the third millennium.

The Changing Minds campaign is trying, in a variety of ways, to encourage everyone to stop and think about their own attitudes and behaviour in relation to plus-size individuals.

At the same time, he said, we need to remind ourselves that, directly or indirectly, some form of problem relating to body-mass affects every family in the United States.

The experience of our patients is that discriminatory attitudes are widespread (again, no pun intended) within the general public, the medical profession, employers, banks, insurance companies and every other organization in America.

Marie Chub, chief executive of the charity SLIM, said: "We hope that the ads from the campaign will help overweight people who so often feel larger than life (once again, no pun intended) and not able to keep up with society to feel that they belong and that someone is there to help.

The charity's helpline, Slimline, can be contacted at 1-800-THINK THIN

*Source: The Mentally Ill Mentor, by David Grant Miller

While *my* fictional "campaign to end the stigma attached to obesity" may sound absurd, it effectively illustrates how counter-productive such a campaign can be. Whether it's Mental Illness or Obesity, the underlying message is loud and clear: *We* will protect you since *you are incapable of protecting yourself.*

CHAPTER 8

Stigma: An Insider's Perspective

THE *REAL* MESSAGE EXPLAINED

In his best-selling book, *The 7 Habits of Highly Effective People*, Dr. Stephen R. Covey shares a personal experience about protection. In his book he describes how he and his wife Sandra protected their "academically and athletically challenged" son from the hurtful comments of his siblings.

STEPHAN COVEY'S STORY

At a baseball game, when their son missed hitting the ball and was teased by his siblings, Dr. and Mrs. Covey would say something like: "Shh! Leave him alone! He's trying his best!" When their son would get ridiculed about a low mark in school, they would also go to great lengths to protect their son from the hurtful comments of his siblings regarding his level of intelligence.

To their surprise, however, the Covey's eventually realized that their protection - a natural outgrowth of love for their child - was very counter productive. Through deep thought and sincere prayer they realized that their protection was sending a very clear message to their son: *You NEED us to protect you, because you REALLY ARE incompetent.*

Recognizing their mistake and being honest about the motives behind their protection, the Covey's realized that their underlying message was flawed. In reality, their son DIDN'T need their protection, because he REALLY WAS competent.

Dr. Covey explains that initially, as he and his wife withdrew their protection, their son suffered some withdrawal pains. But as he became accustomed to protecting *himself* his life underwent a rapid, positive transformation.

His level of self-esteem and self-confidence increased remarkably. He became much happier. And before long, their son's grades improved significantly and he began to *excel* in athletics!

Why?

In his own words, Dr. Covey gives the answer: "Because we saw him as fundamentally adequate and able to cope with life, we stopped protecting him against the ridicule of others." "We don't need to protect you," was the unspoken message. "You're fundamentally okay."

NON-PROTECTION THEORY

As someone who has *personally* struggled with a Mental Illness and has *actually* received protection from others, I am here to tell you that what I call "Non-Protection Theory" is just as true when it comes to Mental Illness.

Just as a "plus-size individual" doesn't need protection, neither does a person with a Mental Illness, assuming the person is not "a danger to him/herself or others." A "plus-size individual" can begin to exercise, eat nutritional meals and cut out junk food and lose the weight they want to. Similarly, a person with a Mental Illness can learn how to take responsibility for themselves and their illness and can eventually overcome it. (We will discuss specific things that can be done, later.)

If you are a family member concerned about a loved one who is struggling with a Mental Illness it may seem as if I am suggesting you should shirk your duty and throw your loved one to the wolves. On the contrary. Assuming your loved one is not "a *danger* to him/herself or others" without it, withdrawing your protection is the most loving, helpful thing you can do.

Just like Stephan and Sandra Covey's son, your lack of protection will go a long way in fostering the *correct* underlying message that your loved one is "fundamentally okay."

MY STORY

During *my* struggle with a Mental Illness, my wife, Aimee, refused to protect *me*. Although I completely disagreed with her and even craved her protection, she remained firm.

In time her underlying message became clear: *Regardless of how you feel right now, you are fundamentally okay. One day you are going to pull out of this depression and make something of your life.*

In a time when I felt hopeless and had little faith in myself, Aimee's belief in me - manifested by her lack of protection - was what kept me going. Just knowing that she believed in me and my ability to be success-ful eventually helped me see that she was right.

PART 4

SECRETS TO SUCCESS

Since taking responsibility for the state of your Mental Health is not always easy, I would like to share with you four secrets. These secrets will help you as you apply principles of good Mental Health in your life. These secrets directly apply to each area discussed later including issues relating to diet, sleep, exercise and releasing stress. Because they are so powerful in helping you *stay* committed to your goal, you may find it helpful to review the secrets periodically.

CHAPTER 1

Secret 1: Have Faith in Yourself & the Program

Now that you have committed – on paper – to overcome your Mental Illness, Secret 1 will help you as you cultivate your belief in yourself and work toward your goal of Mental Wellness.

MY STORY

The other day, while finding a secluded spot in the country to enjoy my lunch, I drove up behind a car that was waiting at a railroad crossing. Like many rural crossings, this one intersected the tracks on a curve. Because of the curve, as well as many trees and an abundance of tall grass, it was almost impossible to see if there was a train approaching. However, judging by the flashing red lights and loud warning bells, I reasoned that there *was* a train coming, and that it would appear in front of us any moment. But after patiently waiting for a few minutes, I began to wonder whether a big, huge hunk of metal was really speeding down the tracks or if the lights were just malfunctioning.

After waiting a few moments longer, I decided it was time to investigate. I backed up, turned my wheel sharply to the left, and slowly crept forward, situating myself beside the car I had been parked behind. To my surprise, I was still unable to determine whether a train was actually approaching. Inching forward until my front bumper was only a few feet from the tracks, I stopped.

Having a clear view of the track, I looked right. I could now see the bare tracks clearly for over a mile. No train. Looking left, however, I discovered that a train was *parked* on the tracks several hundred yards from the crossing. It was so far away, in fact, I estimated that it had just barely tripped the sensor that triggered the annoying, loud bells, and bright red flashing lights.

After quickly driving across the tracks, I looked in my rear-view mirror to see what the car behind me would do. To my surprise, the car sat motionless until it was almost out of my view. Finally, an elderly woman got out, slowly walked up to where I had driven and looked both ways, just as I had done. Being completely sure there was no danger, I watched as she got back in, and the car slowly crept forward and finally crossed the tracks.

As I watched this scene unfold before my eyes, I wondered how long that elderly woman and her husband would have watched the flashing red lights and listened to the incessant clanging of the bells had *I* not made the decision to creep forward and *find out for myself* whether or not there was really any danger of getting plowed by 100,000 tons of steel.

YOU CAN DO IT!

Like me and the couple behind me, many people get stuck waiting at a set of "train tracks" at some point in their lives. When all indications seem to point to a major life-threatening danger ahead, it just seems to make sense to wait and play it safe.

In your life, as the bright red lights continue to flash on and off, and as the sound of the warning bells continues to pierce your ears, remember that the time for waiting is over. You are now ready to cross the tracks and make a new life for yourself.

The great thing is, you don't have to go it alone. I will be with you every step of the way. As you continue to follow me across the tracks and into the "unknown" it will be helpful to simply have faith in the program.

Just believing that the principles and techniques I will introduce you to *will* work for you is half the battle in your quest to make them a part of your life. Second, have faith in *yourself* and *your ability* to achieve Mental Wellness. Third, have faith that God is well aware of you as a person and is very willing to help you. All you have to do is pray and ask.

As you continue to have faith, I encourage you to keep this thought at the forefront of your mind: You CAN do it! Across the tracks, out there in the "unknown", is a life of peace, happiness and success just waiting for you to discover!

CHAPTER 2

Secret 2: Your Oxygen Mask

IMAGINATION ACTIVITY

I magine for a moment that you are on a large jet airplane. As you prepare for takeoff the captain comes over the loudspeaker and announces that it is time to review flight safety procedures. Bored with the demonstrations and explanations already familiar to you from other flights, you pay little attention as a stewardess explains what to do in an emergency, including proper use of your oxygen mask. One of the procedures she highlights is this: in the unlikely event that the air pressure in the cabin of the plane fails, the wearing of an oxygen mask is extremely important. Without it, of course, you would not be able to breathe. Next, the stewardess says something to this effect: "If you are traveling with young children, you must ensure you put *your* oxygen mask on *first.*"

MY STORY

The first time I flew on a large airplane and listened to this instruction, I was puzzled. Why would any loving parent, I wondered, put their child in 2nd place in favour of getting *their* oxygen mask on first? To me it seemed to make more sense to get the mask on my child first. After all, I reasoned, a child has a much lower lung capacity than an adult, and would be less capable of holding their breath while waiting to put an oxygen mask on.

Not until several months after my hospitalizations, however, did I begin to comprehend the deep importance of the principle of putting on your *own* oxygen mask first. I discovered it one evening as I chatted on the phone with an acquaintance who is now a successful Life Coach. We agreed that "putting on your oxygen mask" in everyday life simply meant taking care of your own basic needs on a daily basis. These could include things from exercise to journal writing to eating properly to taking time to meditate and reflect on life. All of these things would improve my Mental Health and increase my level of happiness.

Discussing this principle with my "Coach," Doug, I explained that while I knew "putting on my oxygen mask" was important, with three children, a demanding job, and church responsibilities, it just wasn't possible for me to take time for myself. There were simply too many other priorities.

Luckily for me, Doug was not about to let me blame everyone or everything else for the reason I was constantly starved for air. After showing empathy for my busy life, and recognizing that my children and many other things *should* be high on my priority list, he asked what would happen if I applied my belief to an actual emergency on an airplane. Having never thought about it that way, I ran the scenario through my mind. Then, after a brief pause, it hit me.

"I could pass out before I ever got the oxygen mask on my child!!" I said. "By doing what I perceived was the noble, unselfish thing to do, I could actually put my child's life in jeopardy." Realizing what I had just said, I was shocked at what Doug had led me to discover.

In reality, by sacrificing for my children by always putting their needs ahead of my own, I was neglecting my own basic needs. And in so doing, I was actually doing my children a disservice. Instead of having a father who was full of kindness and caring, they were getting a father who was full of resentment and frustration. Why? I was constantly starved for "air."

LEARN TO PUT ON *YOUR* OXYGEN MASK FIRST

One of the main ways *you* can show love to *yourself* and the people around you is by learning to put on *your* oxygen mask first. Doing so will give you the energy and patience you need to take care of your loved ones with compassion and love. It will also enable you to focus and complete important tasks in all areas of your life.

Applying the "Oxygen Mask Principle" in *my* life has been a significant factor in my success in overcoming *my* Mental Illness. Now, when I am tempted to do things like skipping my morning exercise in favour of taking care of the immediate needs of my family, I stop myself and realize that I will be no good to my family if I am gasping for breath. Instead, by putting on *my* oxygen mask first, I have more patience, and an increased ability to be kind and loving to those I care about most.

If you are struggling with a Mental Illness I am betting that *you* are starving for air. Just like me, you may be accustomed to putting everyone and everything else in your life ahead of your own needs. While this can seem like the noble thing to do, don't be fooled. Nobody but nobody is at their best for others while they, themselves, are starving for air.

By applying Secret 2 in your life, you too, will be able to breathe. As you implement this principle you will feel better about yourself, have more patience, feel less stressed, and feel more capable of taking care of the important people and responsibilities in your life.

CHAPTER 3

Secret 3: Becoming Aware of Crisis! Mode

MY STORY

Anticipating some much-needed sleep, I quietly crawled into bed. As I did, I silently prayed that our baby daughter, whose crib was located right next to our bed, would sleep through the night. Suffering from back pain and feeling exhausted from the day's labors, I was just too tired and sore to deal with her crying.

However, within a few minutes, Julianna did wake up, screaming "Mommy! Mommy!" which I knew was a sure sign that "Daddy" would have no chance at consoling her. So, instead of trying to pull my tired body out of bed to pick her up I waited, confident that Aimee would soon enter the room and rescue me from the noise. Slowly, the minutes ticked by, but still no sign of Aimee. Then, when I was almost ready to shout for Aimee to come and get our screaming daughter, Julianna miraculously fell back asleep. As I continued to lay motionless, I enjoyed the wonderful silence and prayed it would continue.

Unfortunately, just as I was about to drift off I heard "Mommy! Mommy!" again, as Julianna began again to cry and scream. Again, I felt confident that Aimee would come in promptly to allow me to finally get the sleep I was craving. Much to my disappointment, however, after five long minutes, Aimee had still not entered the room. Feeling my level of patience drop like a rock, I decided it was time to give Aimee a piece of my mind. After all, she knew how badly my back hurt, and how desperately I needed sleep. And yet she continued to neglect getting Julianna as she screamed at the top of her lungs even though she knew that she was the only one our baby girl would respond to.

Furious at her level of disrespect toward me, I clenched my teeth, painfully dragged myself out of the bed, stomped into the living room, and gave Aimee the stare of death. As I did, I demanded to know why she had not come to get Julianna when she knew I was in terrible pain and was dead tired.

Proving she had absolutely no compassion for my situation, she *said* that she had not heard Julianna and that she would be in soon. But "soon" was not good enough for me. So, when she declined my request to come "immediately," I clenched my teeth, tightened my fist, and stomped off back towards the bedroom. Then, as my anger built to the point of explosion, I wound up, eyed the perfect spot, and punched a hole right in the middle of our hallway wall!

CRISIS DEFINED

At that moment in time, I was sure I was smack-dab in the middle of a real-for-real crisis situation. But was I?

Well, the dictionary defines "crisis" as: *"an unstable situation of extreme danger or difficulty."* By definition, and by common sense, it is obvious to me now that the situation described above was definitely *not* a crisis. But what bothered me for many months after my wall-punching episode was the question of how I allowed such a minor, common occurrence like our baby daughter crying, to send me into an angry rage.

WHAT IS "CRISIS! MODE?"

"Crisis! Mode," as I like to call it, is simply blowing things out of proportion without realizing what you are doing. When I reacted to Aimee for not getting Julianna right away, it was in the same way I would have reacted if she had just told me she wanted a divorce! Obviously, in this situation, I was in Crisis! Mode.

Another aspect of Crisis! Mode is the magnifying of the negative aspects of a situation almost to the exclusion of the positive. This is almost always accompanied with a large dose of bad attitude. Again, in my case, my focus was completely on me and all the reasons why Aimee should have jumped up to get Julianna the minute I asked her to. Funny thing was, however, I didn't even *think* of checking *Julianna* to see what was wrong with her!! I was so self-absorbed that taking care of *her* immediate needs was the furthest thing from my mind.

Because being in Crisis! Mode is such a common occurrence in our society, regardless of whether a Mental Illness is involved, we will discuss it in more detail a little later. For now, however, just be aware that, like my situation, your mind can kick into Crisis! Mode anytime you *perceive* a crisis - "*an unstable situation of extreme danger or difficulty*". But remember, *believing* you are in the middle of a crisis does not automatically mean that you *actually* are. On the rare occasion when a real-for-real crisis does crop up, staying calm, cool, and collected is a much smarter way to deal with it!

CHAPTER 4

Secret 4: The Power of The 5-Minute Principle

EATING AN ELEPHANT

Have you ever watched the episode of Fear Factor where the contestants are asked to eat an entire elephant all on their own? Me neither. In fact, I don't think such an episode exists.

But what would you do if you were *actually* asked to eat an elephant? Sure, the question sounds funny, but just think about it for a moment. Would you take out your knife and fork and dig in? Or would you decide that your task was too difficult and give up before you even started?

MY STORY

When asked to eat an elephant – or to begin working on what I perceived as a really big task - I used to be the type to give up before even starting. It was just too much work, with too little chance of success. It was too disheartening.

To determine if you need help in the area of "elephant eating," consider the following scenario's and check off the ones that apply:

I often feel overwhelmed when:

__ I look at the pile of dirty dishes stacked by the sink

__ I think of the pile of dirty laundry stacked up by the washer

__ I think about how long it will take me to clean the house and/or garage

__ I think of all the work involved in overcoming my Mental Illness

__ I think of _____

I often feel discouraged when:

__ I think of all my goals

__ I mentally review my financial position

__ I think about the direction my life is headed

__ I think about _____

I often procrastinate:

__ Doing the dishes, the laundry, and/or cleaning the house and/or garage

__ Reviewing and setting new goals

__ Taking action to improve my financial situation

__ Taking steps that will help me create the life I wish I had

__ Doing/taking action on _____

When I was struggling to overcome my Mental Illness, I would have checked off every single item on the list. But now that I am Mentally Well I have adopted a different point of view – one that has helped me to avoid feeling overwhelmed and discouraged. *The Secret? The 5-Minute Principle.*

To the question: *"How do you eat an elephant?"* this principle answers: *"One bite at a time."* In other words, the key to success in accomplishing GIGANTIC tasks, such as eating an elephant, is not to try and do it all at once, but rather, to break it down into bite-sized pieces. Granted, eating an elephant one bite at a time would still take a very, very long time. But if you were to consistently spend 5 minutes every day, eating and chewing just a few bites, you would eventually accomplish the task.

IMPLEMENTING THE 5-MINUTE PRINCIPLE

Unless you are on a very, very long episode of Fear Factor, you will likely never be faced with the real challenge of eating an elephant. But we all encounter daily situations that can seem almost as difficult.

When you feel overwhelmed and discouraged and are tempted to procrastinate doing something that really needs doing, STOP!! Then, *pretend* that you're on Fear Factor, with millions of people watching, and pretend you are *actually* going to begin eating an elephant. Thinking of your ENORMOUS task in this way will help lighten the discouraging atmosphere you have created, while also helping you remember The 5-Minute Principle.

Listed below are three step-by-step suggestions for exactly how to do this:

1. View that huge pile of dishes or laundry or whatever may be your elephant in a different way. Instead of ignoring it, set just 5 minutes on a timer and get to work.

2. Since you are going to be doing the work anyway, put a smile on

your face, start humming your favorite tune, and decide to work hard and be happy until the timer rings.

3. When the timer rings, if you still are "not into" what you are doing, just stop. Then, plan a future time for accomplishing your task. When that time comes, begin again by working hard and being happy about it for only 5 minutes. Chances are, this time you may even feel like sticking it out for a total of ten minutes – double the time you spent originally! (Now that's progress!)

MY SUCCESS CAN BE *YOUR* SUCCESS

Staying focused on accomplishing huge tasks with consistency and a positive attitude is something I once found a little tough. But as I have implemented The 5-Minute Principle I have experienced a new power to get done what needs to be done. From tackling that pile of dirty dishes, to getting out of debt, to overcoming a Mental Illness, implementing The 5-Minute Principle will prove very valuable in every area of *your* life, too.

So from now on, if you begin to feel overwhelmed or discouraged, or if you're tempted to procrastinate a really large undertaking, STOP!! Then remember what you've learned about eating an elephant, put a grin on your face, start humming your favorite tune, and go to work!

CHAPTER 5

Review: You CAN Do It!!

B efore we continue our journey into Part 5, lets review what we have covered. Below is a "Reader's Digest" condensed version of each of the four secrets.

SECRET 1: HAVE FAITH IN THE PROGRAM

Keep Secret 1 in mind as you learn and apply everything you read in this book. For now, just have faith that what I am telling you is true. The key to doing this is mentally preparing yourself for change. In this case, the change will be a smart, well-thought out, calculated risk. Like crossing train tracks when the red lights are flashing and the warning bells are clanging loudly, this may not be an easy step for you. That being said, however, now that you are committed to overcoming your Mental Illness, you will have the power to do it. And, as you begin to live what you have learned, you will discover for yourself that it really works!

SECRET 2: PUTTING ON *YOUR* OXYGEN MASK FIRST

Secret 2 has everything to do with making YOU a priority in your life. Acknowledgement and action is the key to making this secret a part of your life. In other words, you can acknowledge that, while you have the demands of children or work or whatever it may be, YOU matter. Instead of continuing to gasp for air, Secret 2 involves taking action by putting on *your* "oxygen mask" first. As you take time out for *yourself* on a *daily* basis, you will be much more capable of taking care of all the other important people and priorities in your life.

SECRET 3: BECOMING AWARE OF CRISIS! MODE

Just like *me* over-reacting to our crying baby daughter, *you* may be over-reacting to normal, every day situations in your life. If you are, there is a good chance you are in "Crisis! Mode." While we will discuss how to get out of Crisis! Mode later, for now, just becoming aware of your tendency to see a Crisis! in every situation will help you to relax and calm down.

SECRET 4: THE POWER OF THE 5-MINUTE PRINCIPLE

When it comes to large, potentially discouraging tasks, just remember Secret 4, the secret to "eating an elephant." By breaking huge tasks into bite-sized pieces, your ability to focus and be happy about potentially overwhelming tasks will be significantly increased.

With these important secrets in mind, it is time to move on to learning more about their practical application in your life.

• • •

The rest of *The Mentally Ill Mentor* discusses four main areas that relate to your goal of creating and maintaining long term Mental Wellness:

1. Understanding why you may be stuck in Crisis! Mode, and how to get out of it.

2. Changing the way you view yourself.

3. Unconditionally loving and accepting YOU just the way you are, right at this moment.

4. Respecting and fulfilling your body's basic needs.

Applying the wisdom of the Four Secrets to each of these areas will enable you to develop the courage and self-confidence you need to successfully achieve your goal of Life-Long Mental Wellness.

PART 5

GETTING OUT OF CRISIS! MODE

• • •

If you have been stuck in "Crisis! Mode", as so many people with a Mental Illness are, applying these principles will enable you to lower your level of stress and allow you to begin enjoying the calm, peaceful life you want and deserve.

• • •

CHAPTER 1

Am I Really in Crisis! Mode?

BAD NEWS/GOOD NEWS

Not everyone in Crisis! Mode has a Mental Illness. But in my experience, nearly everyone with a Mental Illness is in Crisis! Mode. Why? Perceiving a Crisis! – "an unstable situation of extreme danger or difficulty" – in every situation enables a person with a Mental Illness to postpone making important, difficult decisions. In a nutshell, experiencing the world in Crisis! Mode is an escape – a way to procrastinate dealing with reality. That's the bad news.

The good news is, now that you are aware that you may have a problem, you can now take steps to solve it.

SELF-EVALUATION

Before you can effectively work your way out of Crisis! Mode, it is important to first determine what end of the Crisis! Mode spectrum you are on. Are you the type of person who freaks out at every little thing? Or, does it take an issue of some significance before you get really worked up and bent out of shape?

This simple test will give you a good idea. Check off those that apply to you.

__ I often feel as if I am overloaded with stress

__ I am often irritable

__ I wake up each morning anticipating that many things will go wrong with my day

__ I often become angry with the actions of others, but do not communicate my feelings

__ I long for a break from the stresses I encounter on a daily basis, but rarely take one

__ I am easily annoyed with the mistakes of others

__ My level of patience with my children needs improvement

__ I often feel guilt, shame and regret because of the way I treat my children and others

__ I often feel angry and annoyed with my husband or wife, and even myself

__ I look down on people who always seem calm and peaceful

__ I view calm and peaceful people as being out-of-touch with reality

__ I believe in the saying "Life's tough and then you die"

__ I rarely smile, laugh, make jokes or find any aspect of my life humorous

__ I often use extreme words such as "desperate", "mortified" and "excruciating"

__ I often use words such as "can't", "have to", and "beyond my control", to describe my less-than-desirable situations in my life

__ I have HUGE issues with people not being on time

__ I do not enjoy trying to accommodate the schedules of others

__ I feel like a fish out of water unless I am constantly busy

To score your test, simply consider the following: The more items checked off, the deeper your problem with Crisis! Mode. But wait! Even if you checked off every single item, there is no need to fly off the handle! Just take a few deep breaths, remain calm, and come with me as we continue the next leg of our journey: Understanding and getting out of Crisis! Mode. ☺

CHAPTER 2

Understanding Crisis! Mode

Perhaps the biggest secret to getting out of Crisis! Mode relates to Secret 2: Putting Your Oxygen Mask On First, and the idea that taking care of *you* is important.

In the last chapter, you checked off symptoms of Crisis! Mode that apply to you. Now that we have established the existence and depth of your problem, it will also be helpful for you to understand the reasons behind it.

IT'S A "MULTI-FACTORIAL THING"

In analyzing my behavior since I punched the hole in our hallway wall, I have come to the realization that Crisis! Mode is, what I like to call, a "Multi-Factorial Thing." In other words, there are usually not one, but several reasons behind a constant perception of the existence of a crisis. While the following list is not exclusive, listed below are three factors that are important to recognize.

FACTOR # 1: GOOD OL' CHILDHOOD EXPERIENCES

While we have already discussed the importance of letting go of childhood issues, understanding how and where you learned about what constitutes a Crisis! in the first place is key in fixing the problem. To that end, answer the following questions:

•   Do you remember being spanked or scolded as a child and being told what a "bad girl" or "bad boy" you were after making simple mistakes like spilling milk, wrecking a houseplant, or denting the family car?

•   As a child, did you witness frequent and/or intense, heated arguments between your parents?

•   Growing up, did your mother and/or father worry excessively?

Unfortunately, for most people, negative childhood experiences such as the ones I have mentioned have made significant contributions to being in Crisis! Mode in adulthood. However, as we have already discussed, blaming your childhood will do no good in getting out of Crisis! Mode. Taking responsibility for the way things are now, will.

FACTOR # 2: ACCUMULATION OF STRESS

The fact that accumulation of stress can significantly contribute to your being in Crisis! Mode probably comes as no surprise to you. However, what is surprising, is how many people - with and without a Mental Illness - continue to wallow in their self-created misery without making any attempt to change their situation or lower their level of stress.

To determine if an accumulation of stress is contributing to your being in Crisis! Mode ask yourself some more questions in the following key areas:

- **Key Relationships:** Am I unhappy in my relationship with my husband or wife, my significant other, my children, or other key people in my life?

- **Employment**: Do I feel ongoing stress in relation to my job?

- **Living Conditions**: Do I enjoy living in the neighborhood, city, state, or country in which I currently reside? Do I enjoy living in my home?

FACTOR # 3: IGNORING YOUR INNER VOICE

Did your "Inner Voice" speak to you as you asked yourself the questions above? Did it tell you it was time for a change? If it did, what was your reaction to it?

Although you may have become accustomed to ignoring your Inner Voice, it often imparts wisdom that, if listened to, can be really beneficial to you in terms of the ways you can work to improve your life. The great thing is, if paid attention to and acted on, the wisdom of our Inner Voice will show us how to find the inner peace and serenity we are all searching for.

With an understanding of why you are stuck in Crisis! Mode, you are ready to take the next step of learning how to get out of it.

CHAPTER 3

Getting Out of Crisis! Mode

Now that we have discussed three contributing factors to Crisis! Mode, lets get on with practical solutions. To do this, keep these three simple questions in mind anytime you perceive a potential "Crisis!."

1. **Ask Yourself**: Does this situation qualify as real-for-real "crisis": Is it really and truly *"an unstable situation of extreme danger or difficulty"?* If your answer is "no," consider the possibility that *you are unstable, extreme, or making the situation difficult.*

2. **Ask Yourself**: In an hour, a day, a week, a month, a year, or at the end of your life, will this issue really matter?

3. **Ask Yourself**: Will going into "Crisis! Mode" by focusing on all the negative aspects of the situation, almost to the exclusion of the positive, help you to work through the situation in the most effective and efficient way?

SOLUTION # 1: GOOD OL' CHILDHOOD EXPERIENCES

*   Question: Do you remember being disciplined and told what a bad girl or boy you were after doing something like spilling milk, wrecking a house plant or denting the family car?

Now, lets analyze this situation with the three questions in mind:

1. **Does this situation qualify as real-for-real "crisis": "*an unstable situation of extreme danger or difficulty*"?** While you may have adopted a false belief taught by your parents, spilling milk, wrecking a house plant or denting the family car (no matter how expensive) definitely does NOT constitute a crisis.

2. **In an hour, a day, a week, a month, a year, or at the end of your life, will this issue really matter?** Short answer: NO!

3. **Will going into "Crisis! Mode" positively affect the outcome of this situation?** Obviously not.

Analysis: *Over-reacting by going into Crisis! Mode is very counter-productive. It can create feelings of fear and inadequacy in children. It can also lead to children growing up with the false belief that the normal accidents and mistakes are a really big deal. It can also lead to more overreacting about even more issues.*

YOUR TURN

With these three questions in mind, analyze for yourself the rest of the questions posed under Factor # 1: Good ol' Childhood experiences.

FACTOR # 2: ACCUMULATION OF STRESS

If you answered "yes!" to any of the following questions, and have become converted to the idea of getting out of "Crisis! Mode," the following suggestions will help:

- **Key Relationships:** Am I unhappy in my relationship with my husband or wife, significant other, or our children?

If your key relationships are an ongoing source of stress, the answer lies in simply dealing with the problem effectively. Doing this can include simple things like taking time to communicate your feelings, reading and discussing books, such as John Gray's *Men Are From Mars, Women Are From Venus,* and/or discussing problems with a professional relationship counselor.

- **Employment:** Do I feel ongoing stress in relation to my job?

I often wonder why so many people stay in jobs that bring them little satisfaction and are the cause of such an enormous amount of stress. These are the people who hate nightshift, but work it often. They are also the ones who despise being in the presence of every one of their co-workers, but don't ever quit and move on. If this is the case for you, it is high time to make some important changes. No matter how bad you *think* things will be if you make major changes, by researching alternatives and planning ahead, you can prepare yourself to take the plunge. From personal experience I can tell you that doing so will go a long way in helping you achieve a state of inner peace and serenity.

- **Living Conditions:** Do I enjoy living in the neighborhood, city, state, or country in which I reside? Do I enjoy living in my home?

Bottom Line: If anything about where you live is a major source of stress, do what you can to change it. If that doesn't work, move. Even though doing so may be difficult, the reward of a more calm, peaceful life will be well worth it!

OK, BUT WHAT ABOUT A "REAL-FOR-REAL" CRISIS!?

First, there are precious few situations that qualify as a real-for-real crisis.

However, in real crisis situations - like the Tsunami in South Asia, or the attacks on the World Trade Centers, or when a person wants to commit suicide - the key to effectively dealing with the situation is to *stay out of Crisis! Mode*. In a *real* tragic emergency, doctors, nurses, paramedics, and other emergency workers know that remaining calm is imperative. As you do the same, by keeping your fear in check, you will be able to think much more clearly about the most effective way to deal with the situation.

If you have been stuck in "Crisis! Mode," as so many people with a Mental Illness are, applying the principles we have just discussed will enable you to lower your level of stress and allow you to begin enjoying the calm, peaceful life you want and deserve.

PART 6
WHAT ARE YOU REALLY WORTH?

———————————

• • •

Now that you are committed to long term Mental Wellness and creating for yourself a happy, successful life, recognizing your intrinsic and infinite worth as a Child of God will help you in accomplishing your goal.

• • •

CHAPTER 1

The Worth of a Soul

MY STORY

A few years ago I decided that the most logical way to deal with my deep self-hate and unsolvable problems was to end it all. I reasoned that my children would no longer have to deal with a poor role model. My wife would finally be out of perpetual poverty with the money from my life insurance policy, which I knew included suicide. In fact, everyone I knew would finally be rid of me – an annoying thorn in their sides. It all seemed right. It was a calculated, intelligent decision based purely on logic.

But as I began to envision myself going downstairs to get my gun... something stopped me and told me what I was doing was wrong!! I felt as if someone was wrapping a warm blanket around my cold and troubled soul and assuring me everything would be alright. When I least expected it, through some miracle, I began to see how off-base my "intelligent logic" was. I began to understand that even *I* was worth something to God – if not even to myself.

As I struggled through the next few years, slowly but surely, the way I viewed myself began to improve. At one point, while visiting a local business, I noticed a piece of paper pinned on the Director's wall. The words on the page seemed to speak to my soul, and I requested a copy. Reading that "writing on the wall" has forever altered the way I think about myself. It has also increased my ability to understand my true potential and the potential of every other human being.

As it relates to your quest to create and maintain long term Mental Wellness, I urge you to think deeply about what you are about to read. The concepts presented are simple yet powerful and they can help you in ways you may never have thought possible.

OUR GREATEST FEAR

Our greatest fear is not that we are inadequate,
but that we are powerful beyond measure.

It is our light, not our darkness, that frightens us.
We ask ourselves, Who am I to be brilliant,
gorgeous, handsome, talented and fabulous?

Actually, who are you not to be?
You are a child of God.

Your playing small does not serve the world.
There is nothing enlightened about shrinking
so that other people won't feel insecure around you.

We were born to make manifest the glory of God within us.
It is not just in some; it is in everyone.

And, as we let our own light shine, we consciously give

other people permission to do the same.
As we are liberated from our fear,
our presence automatically liberates others.

Source: *A Return to Love*, by Marianne Williamson

These words encompass the essence of what God thinks of us and speaks to what our potential truly is *regardless of whether we believe it or not*.

For me, it took being dangerously close to taking my own life before I truly began to understand my importance and worth in the eyes of God. As I began to comprehend *His* love for me, I was able to begin to show this love to *myself*. When we are committed to Life - Long Mental Wellness and creating a happy, successful life, recognizing our intrinsic and infinite worth as a Child of God will help us accomplish our goals. It will also improve our perception of ourselves and our capabilities.

CHAPTER 2

The Great Untruth

IMAGINE THIS: NELSON MANDELA WITH NO SELF WORTH

After spending 27 years in jail and tirelessly working toward what he believed in, the now famous Nelson Mandela went on to become the President of South Africa and establish equal rights for all people in that country. That is what *actually* happened.

But imagine for a moment how his life – and the course of history – could have been changed for the worse had he not understood his true worth.

Nelson Mandela's inner thoughts after only serving two of 27 years in prison *could have been* something like this:

I am absolutely fed up with this place. What on earth have I done?! If I would have just kept my mouth shut none of this ever would have happened! Who do I think I am - believing I can help change the thinking of an entire country? Equal rights in this country are just a hollow dream. There will always be slavery. There will always be inequality. Peace, harmony, democracy and equality is impossible. I feel so hopeless! Why couldn't they have just sentenced me to death?!

When you look at it that way, it's easy to see that Mandela could not possibly have achieved what he did if he did not truly understand *his* worth and potential.

"Well," you may be saying to yourself, "That's great for Nelson Mandela, but *I'm* not like him. I *really am* good for nothing. My life *really is* worthless." If you still believe that, I have a good idea of how you must feel. I used to believe the very same thing.

Since becoming Mentally Well, however, I have realized the untruth of those statements. But what I have also become aware of is the huge number of people in this world - both those with and without a Mental Illness - who actually believe statements like that are true! This fact has caused me to ask questions like: "How, when and why, did I and all these people begin to believe what I like to call the "Great Untruth"? While the answer to that question could be extensive enough to be the subject of an entire book, what follows is a short explanation.

HOW, WHEN, WHY?

In childhood we all form beliefs about ourselves. Whether true or false we continue to carry these beliefs with us for the rest of our lives. Because they are so much a part of us, they directly affect the way we see the world. The initial formation of these beliefs is influenced heavily by the beliefs, actions and attitudes of our parents and other primary caregivers.

A WORD ABOUT CHILDHOOD

Despite their best efforts, none of our parents were perfect – mine included. So, while they wanted the best for us, Mom and Dad raised us the only way they knew how - in much the same way that they were raised. In many cases, that "way" was far less than ideal. In childhood, many of us misinterpreted the less-than-loving actions of our parents as: "You are incapable and worthless."

Take, for example, your mother yelling at you for spilling milk all over the floor. When she told you what a "bad" two-year-old girl you were, you likely believed her. After all, she was your *mother*, the very one who gave you life, the one you trusted to take care of all your physical and emotional needs.

When your father got angry with you for scratching the paint on his new car and said things like: "You stupid kid! How could you do such a thing?! Why do I put up with you? All you ever do is cause me grief!" – you may have unconsciously been trying to come up with the answers to his questions. Your internal dialogue may have gone something like this:

He's right! I must be stupid. How could I do such a thing if I wasn't stupid? Why does Dad put up with me? Maybe it's only because he knows he could go to jail if he threw me out on the street. I feel so bad for being such a burden to him. It seems like he is always angry with me.

For me, recalling common childhood experiences such as these stir up deep and sometimes painful emotions and feelings. While I consider my mother and father to be on the kind end of the parenting-style spectrum, when it came to raising me, they, too, were less than perfect. And even though my parents always *told* me that I could do anything I put my mind to, years of childhood "misinterpretation" of their anger and frustration often contradicted what they said. After leaving home to make my own way in life I encountered many situations which seemed to support my false beliefs about myself and my worth.

As I struggled through life, continuing to feel that I was "nothing special," convinced I was fundamentally inadequate in many ways, the frustration that accompanied my feelings of low self-worth eventually came to a head when I realized their source. I finally came to the conclusion that my parents were to blame!

As I pondered more and more on this new theory, I spent many hours mentally reviewing enormous amounts of evidence which supported my belief! I discussed my views with my wife and argued my case unceasingly. In analyzing every failed opportunity or small misfortune, *everything* seemed to somehow have its roots in the way I was raised. I felt sorry that I had been cursed with such an inadequate father and unkind mother. If I would have only had better parents, I rationalized, my adult life would be a whole lot better.

CHAPTER 3

The Blame Game

PLAYING THE BLAME GAME

For many years into my marriage, I continued to play The Blame Game. Occasionally, close friends, siblings and other relatives would join in the game as we discussed how unfortunate our lives were as a result of being raised by such incompetent parents. While I knew deep down that playing the game was wrong - even destructive - I continued to blame them for my problems.

BLAME GAME STRATEGY

If you are a big Blame Game player, I want to let you in on a secret. Although I wasn't born when my parents were newly married, I found an old journal my mother kept from those days. In it, she describes her thoughts and feelings about me – their first child – and the way they intended to raise me. If your parents were as bad at raising you as mine were at raising me, I think you will find the contents of this *private document* to be *very* interesting. Here is just one excerpt:

August 27, 1973

Being pregnant sure isn't all it is cracked up to be. My ankles are swollen, my hips hurt, and I wish like heck that little person would hurry up and make his way out of my body.

Like I was saying to Hank the other night, I sure am anxious for this little thing to be born, even though it will probably be another two months. He agreed, that regardless of whether it is a girl or a boy we should pick a name that it will really dislike – preferably one that is hard to spell and one that everyone at school can make fun of.

But heck, I'm getting ahead of myself. What I'm really excited for is to see if it has his Dad's big, huge, ugly nose! That would be so funny! If it was a girl and that happened, I would be able to teach her about the fact that girls with large shnozes are really ugly. That way, she would never get too stuck on herself!

If it's a boy, I hope he is really scrawny and has a deformed face like Hank's Uncle Bob. Bob has got to be the most goofy looking accident that ever fell out of heaven! If I had a kid like that I'd let him know he was a worthless piece of dirt right from the start, and I would make darn sure to raise him so that he never forgets it!

REALITY CHECK

Okay – before you begin thinking I had a horrible mother, the above "journal entry" was completely made up! My point in sharing this with you is to help you to understand how obvious it is that almost no parent would ever *plan* to "ruin" their children's lives through poor parenting. In my case, regardless of how my parents raised me and what I used to think they "put me through," I am certain that they, along with nearly every parent that has ever lived, didn't ever *intend* to make the mistakes they made.

The truth is, nearly all parents set out to raise their children with good and even noble intentions. They want the very best for their children and they try as best as they know how to give their children the love and attention they need. That you may believe they have failed – even failed miserably – does not negate the fact that they gave it their best shot.

CHAPTER 4

Exploring Forgiveness

YOU ARE A CHILD OF GOD

If you really think about it, being a Child of God means that we are all brothers and sisters. That being the case, I think it is important to know that as a brother, I can relate somewhat to the sense of hurt and anger you may have toward your parents. However, if you were raised in an atmosphere of neglect or abuse, I admit that I have don't any idea of how deep or intense your feelings of hatred and sorrow are.

While it isn't helpful to harbor anger towards our parents it can seem quite natural. But when we are constantly engaged in playing the "Blame Game," those feelings consume us. By continuing to play the game, we constantly re-live past experiences and *continue* to feel the hurt we felt as children. Doing this will just make life miserable.

If you want that misery to remain in your life then playing the "Blame Game" will definitely do it for you. But if you have had enough of the bitterness and anger, enough of the misery, and if you are ready to move on, I am ready to show you how.

WRITING ACTIVITY – YOUR RELATIONSHIP WITH YOUR PARENTS (OR OTHER KEY CAREGIVERS)

Take a minute to fill in the blanks. Feel free to expand on anything on a separate sheet of paper.

Mom

1. My mother is (was) a very _____ woman.

2. The thing I remember most from childhood about my mother is _____

3. When I would do something wrong, my mother would _____ _____

4. Three words that best describe my mother are:

   a. _____

   b. _____

   c. _____

5. Three words that best describe my relationship with my mother are:

   a. _____

   b. _____

   c. _____

6. When I think about my mother I feel _____

7. If I never saw my mother again I would feel _____

8. If I could change one thing about my mother it would be _____ _____

9. If I could go back and change one thing about my relationship with my mother it would be _____

10. I currently believe I am capable of forgiving my mother:
    __ Yes __ No

Dad

11. My father is (was) a very _____ man.

12. The thing I remember most from childhood about my father is _____

13. When I would do something wrong, my father would _____
    _____

14. Three words that best describe my father are:

    a. _____

    b. _____

    c. _____

15. Three words that best describe my relationship with my father are:

    a. _____

    b. _____

    c. _____

16. When I think about my father I feel _____

17. If I never saw my father again I would feel _____

18. If I could change one thing about my father it would be _____
    _____

19. If I could go back and change one thing about my relationship with my father it would be _____

20. I believe I am capable of forgiving my father:

___Yes ___ No

_____ (insert name of someone other than your parents who hurt you deeply in the past)

21. My _____is (was) a very _____ woman/man.

22. The thing I remember most from childhood about _____ is

_____

23. When I would do something wrong, my _____ would _____

_____

24. Three words that best describe my _____ are:

   a. _____

   b. _____

   c. _____

25. Three words that best describe my relationship with my _____ are:

   a. _____

   b. _____

   c. _____

26. When I think about my _____ I feel _____

_____

27. If I never saw _____ again I would feel _____

28. If I could change one thing about my _____ it would be _____

_____

29. If I could go back and change one thing about our relationship it would be _____

30. I currently believe I am capable of forgiving my _____:

    Yes __ No__

    Now, pull out some paper and a pen and take a few minutes to write a few sentences, paragraphs or even pages about your mother and/or your father or other key caregivers. You may also want to write about someone else from your childhood who may have hurt you deeply. This "journal entry" is completely private, and there are no rules, so write down anything and everything that *you* feel is important. Make sure to include your feelings of anger as well as possible hatred and sorrow. For now, make it as mean and nasty as you want. Remember – nobody but you will ever read it.

CHAPTER 5

The Power of Forgiving Your Parents

E ven though the title refers only to parents, this chapter applies
to forgiving anyone from your past who may have hurt you
deeply.

FOLLOW-UP: WRITING ACTIVITY

Doing the writing activity outlined in the last chapter represents your
opportunity to "vent" about your childhood in a *healthy* way. But why
is this important? Simple. While almost everyone I know regularly com-
plains about some aspect of their childhood, I know of very few who
ever take the time and make a concerted effort to actually *resolve* their
feelings. Believe it or not, just writing them out and seeing them on
paper is extremely therapeutic, and may well give you the emotional
release your soul is hungering for.

Now that you have done this activity, take some time to think about
what you have written. Think about the experiences that have brought
you so much pain. Don't dwell on them for too long, but just acknowledge the hurt and allow yourself to validate your own feelings.

After taking as much time as you need – hours, days or weeks, pull
out your journal again and write the following:

I _____, acknowledge the hurt I felt as a child as a result of the painful experiences I have written down. I feel sorrow for myself, but recognize that it is now time to move on and stop letting these experiences hold me back in life.

I now freely forgive my mother and/or father (or another person) for all that they did or did not do when I was growing up. I now *permanently* release my feelings of hurt, anger, sorrow and pain, and choose from this time forward to create for myself a *new* life filled with peace, happiness and joy.

• • •

_____

AN IMPORTANT NOTE

"Deep hurt" can obviously mean very different things for different people. What *I* consider "deep hurt" may not even compare to the depth of *your* pain. I mention this because, when it comes to Mental Illness, I have come to understand that childhood physical and/or sexual abuse can be a significant contributing factor. While I cannot empathize with how you feel, my heart goes out to you, and it truly saddens me that you endured this kind of terrible hardship.

If you have been physically and/or sexually abused and have not yet begun to deal with your feelings, I urge you to begin. And, while reading *The Mentally Ill Mentor* will go a long way in helping you learn how to love yourself and overcome the hurt you feel, I also encourage you to discuss your feelings with a professional counselor – one that is right for *you*. As I have observed people who have done this, I have become a big believer that it is very effective and can be a great help in healing deep and painful wounds.

...

MY STORY

Now that you are serious about Life-Long Mental Wellness, forgiveness of your parents and others is *absolutely essential*. My experience of forgiving my parents began with feelings of intense anger and deep sorrow. But as I continued through the entire process of acknowledging – and thereby validating – my *own* feelings, I felt as if a huge weight was lifted off my shoulders.

Because of this and other important life changes I will discuss later, my relationship with my mother and father has never been better. Now, I can honestly say that I have forgiven them for the mistakes I felt they made in raising me. But more than that, my forgiveness has helped me to understand the truth about my childhood. I *now* understand that my *perception* of how poorly my parents treated me was a little off. Instead, I recognize that my childhood feelings of unjust treatment were greatly magnified by my *adult* feelings of inadequacy and my *own* tendency to treat *myself* harshly.

PART 7:
THE BEAUTY OF BEING TRUE TO YOURSELF

• • •

Just as forgiveness of your parents is absolutely essential, forgiving *yourself* is crucial in regaining your emotional and mental stability.

• • •

CHAPTER 1

The Power of Forgiving Yourself

MY STORY

When I was a new father, Aimee and I took our oldest son (and only child at the time) to the beach. Wanting to have some fun with our little one-year-old, I decided to take him out to play in the water. As I carried Thomas out into the man-made lake, I determined that even at the deepest point, the lake was fairly shallow, and I decided to carry him to the playground on the opposite shore.

As we approached the centre of the lake, the water inched closer and closer to my mouth and nose. It was much deeper than I had first thought, and I realized that I would need to swim for just five or ten feet. Confident in my ability as a swimmer, I held my arm across Thomas's chest and kicked my legs as fast as I could. I felt sure that I could easily and quickly make it across the deepest point of the small lake and once again be able to touch the bottom.

Without weighing the risks involved, I quickly swam 15 feet – much further than I thought I needed to in order to touch bottom. To my surprise, however, I discovered that I couldn't touch. Deciding that I had simply overestimated the distance by a few feet, I swam another 10 feet.

But as I grabbed Thomas by his armpits and began to try to stand up a second time, I quickly realized that I *still* was not able to touch! Beginning to panic, I caught my breath and continued swimming as a feeling of intense fear washed over me. I frantically swam another 10 feet, feeling very tired and out of breath. Thankfully, the next time I put my feet down, I touched bottom. Problem was, my feet only touched when my head was under the water!

Panicking, I pushed off the bottom of the lake, came up for a big breath of air and tried again to swim to shallower water. So tired I felt as if I could barely move, I did the only thing I could think of. I hoisted Thomas high above my head so that at least *he* would be able to breathe, took a deep breath, and went back under the water.

When I came up for air, for what could have been the last time ever, I somehow mustered the energy to swim just two or three more feet. I took another deep breath and again hoisted Thomas over my head, allowing him to breathe. I decided that when I came back up I would try to scream for help.

I tried to touch one last time. I felt my feet make contact with the sand, my head *just* far enough out of the water that I could touch and breathe at the same time! As soon as we were close enough, Thomas, oblivious to our near–death–experience, happily wandered over to the playground and began to play.

HOW DO YOU FORGIVE YOURSELF FOR THAT?!

To this day, I can still recall my intense feelings of regret and shame knowing that my carelessness had almost led to the drowning of our only child. At the time I was convinced that I was the most neglectful and irresponsible father on the planet! But after years of harboring these bad feelings toward myself, I realized that I was not doing anyone any good. Yes, it was irresponsible. Yes, it was unwise. Yes, it was a dumb risk. But regardless of how big the mistake, I came to the conclusion that I would not be able to love myself and move on with my life until I forgave *me*.

So, as I began the process of forgiving others, I made sure to include all the bad feelings I had toward *myself*. Now that I have forgiven myself, I no longer beat myself up for what happened.

CHAPTER 2

The 3 Steps to Forgiving Yourself

STEP 1: UNDERSTAND THAT MISTAKES ARE INEVITABLE

Imagine for a moment watching a little 12-month-old-baby learning to walk. Picture the smile on her face as she takes her first few steps, eager for the approval of her mother and father. Now imagine that, instead of praising her, her mother shakes her head and says: "You bonehead! Every time you try to stand up you just fall right back down! Boy, are you ever an idiot! Why can't you get it right?! You are so dumb! You are never going to succeed! In fact, you'll be lucky if you learn to walk by the time you're 12 years old!!"

Can you imagine a parent saying that to their child? I hope not!!

Even though as adults we are "all grown up" now, in a way, deep down inside, we are just like the children we used to be. And, just like little children, we are still likely to fail before we succeed. As bad as you may feel, however, the fact of the matter is that we are *all* learning. The important part is that we keep trying.

STEP 2: UNDERSTAND YOUR INFINITE WORTH AND POTENTIAL

Just as you are the child of an earthly father, you are also the child of a Heavenly Father. And, as the saying goes: "God don't make no junk." You *really are* a person of infinite worth and you *really do* have limit-less potential. The key to tapping into that potential is becoming so converted to the idea of loving and believing in yourself and your abilities that it becomes a natural part of who you are. When you reach the point that you can truly feel that way about yourself, you will be capable of accomplishing anything you set your mind to!

STEP 3: LET IT GO

Imagination Activity

Picture in your mind being a little child and feeling very hurt by something. Then, think for a moment about how many hurtful experiences you have experienced up to this point in your life. If you are anything like me, I would guess that this number could be somewhere in the hundreds or thousands over the course of your lifetime. Now, take each one of those hurtful experiences and assign them a weight. A small hurtful experience could be assigned a weight of a few ounces. Something more hurtful could be more like 5 pounds or even more. Now, mentally calculate the total combined "weight" of all these experiences.

What "emotional weight" you are currently carrying?

This simple analogy illustrates this point: The cumulative total of all our negative feelings towards ourselves or others can be enormous. Like thousands of pounds resting on our shoulders, our souls can become heavy from the emotional burden we constantly carry with us.

The best way to deal with your "emotional weight" is to simply get rid of it!

One way to do this is to picture in your mind all that weight being lifted off your shoulders by a large industrial crane. Imagine the crane lifting the enormous weight and dropping it into a deep pit in the middle of a secluded desert. Finally, visualize the hole being completely filled up with dirt, covered over, and forgotten about forever.

In visualizing this, I hope you feel an emotional release similar to the one I felt after getting rid of my emotional weight. No longer feeling burdened with regret, sorrow, and shame, I was able to take a giant leap forward in forgiving and forgetting about hurtful experiences from my past. As you release your emotional weight, you, too, will be more capable of loving yourself and others. Doing this will ultimately lead you to a greater level of inner peace, joy and happiness.

CHAPTER 3

Understanding Unconditional Self-Acceptance

MY STORY

When I left home at 19 to serve a mission for my church, my feelings of self-worth were low. As a result, the first few months were a bit rough. I often felt deep feelings of inadequacy which led me to question whether I should continue for the remainder of my two years.

A LIFE-CHANGING MEETING

Focusing almost exclusively on my weaknesses, I became concerned when I discovered that a religious leader I highly respected was coming to the Australian city I was serving in. Over the next few weeks, instead of eagerly anticipating his visit, I became increasingly worried as I thought about how inadequate I would feel in the presence of such an important, righteous man.

When the day of his visit arrived I desperately wanted to enjoy my once-in-a-lifetime experience. But try as I might, I felt powerless in overcoming my fear. Such a man of God, I believed, would see right through me and pick up on all the faults and sins I was preoccupied with.

Respectfully rising with the rest of the large audience as the man entered the room, I felt so small, so insignificant and so unworthy I wanted to hide. And, as he began shaking hands with everyone in the room I became terrified knowing that my turn was next.

Finally, he stopped in front of me. As I extended my arm and shook his hand, the most amazing feeling came over me. My sense of unworthiness and inadequacy melted away and I was enveloped by a warm, peaceful feeling unlike anything I had ever felt before.

Looking back, it was in that moment that I began to comprehend my value in the eyes of God. If this man could accept me despite all my faults, I reasoned, I was capable of doing the same thing. I also began to understand *God's* love and unconditional acceptance of me.

CHAPTER 4

Unconditionally Accepting & Loving YOU

ACCEPT YOURSELF JUST THE WAY YOU ARE

After forgiveness, the next step is accepting *yourself* just the way you are. Like a child who stumbles and falls but gets back up and keeps on trying, unconditional acceptance of *yourself,* regardless of your level of success, is crucial. Beating yourself up for making mistakes is unfair and unproductive. Instead, treat yourself gently as you continue to learn life skills one step at a time.

HER STORY

Once upon a time there was a sweet little baby born in a small town in Alabama. This little girl was not much different than other little girls her age until she became very ill a few months before her second birthday. The strange illness tormented her, and although she lived through it, her mother soon realized that she no longer heard the dinner bell, nor responded to anything around her. Sadly, in time the mother realized the little girl had become deaf. This made it extremely difficult for her to learn to speak. On top of that, her mother also discovered that she was blind!

In the years that followed, this sweet little girl turned into a monster. She began smashing dishes and lamps as part of her extreme temper tantrums. Her relatives even suggested to the little girl's parents that she needed to be institutionalized. Thankfully, however, the little girl's parents believed in their daughter's intrinsic worth and her ability to be successful regardless of her current situation and outrageous behavior.

• • •

Through a series of events, including consultation with Alexander Graham Bell, the family of the little girl decided to hire a tutor who could relate to what their seven-year-old daughter was going through. The tutor was also deaf and blind.

SUCCESS

For the first few weeks the little girl tried the patience of her tutor as she continued to resist being disciplined. She continued to do "unthinkable" things like eating dinner with her hands and stealing food off every one else's plates. But despite her out-of-control behavior, the deaf and blind teacher persisted.

Eventually her persistence paid off, and the little girl began to comprehend and understand language at an incredible rate. By the time she was 10 she began to speak. She continued to persist in communicating verbally even when others had difficulty understanding her.

As a woman, she eventually learned four languages in Braille, and by the age of 20, entered Radcliffe College, the women's branch of Harvard University. She wrote 11 books, the first of which was translated into 50 languages.

But her accomplishments didn't end there. She engaged in extensive research and fundraising for the blind. She traveled the world giving speeches and inspiring millions. She also won many awards along the way, including the Presidential Medal of Freedom, the highest honor an American civilian can receive.

Beginning with a mother and father who unconditionally accepted and loved their daughter, Helen Keller became empowered with the ability to show the same unconditional acceptance and love to *herself*. In so doing, she was able to tap into her potential, and live a life that would be considered great by any standard.

PART 8

TAKING CARE OF YOUR EMOTIONAL NEEDS

In Parts 6 and 7 we discussed the importance of loving and unconditionally accepting yourself. Coming to a deep understanding of these principles will lay the foundation for what we will discuss next. In Part 8, you will become empowered as you engage yourself in following the easy-to-follow Three-Step Program I will describe. Taking care of your mental, emotional and physical needs will enable you to further build upon your foundation of self-love and unconditional self-acceptance. These steps will help you achieve a life of peace and happiness that includes sustained Mental Wellness. So let's begin.

STEP 1

BECOMING YOUR OWN BEST FRIEND

CHAPTER 1

The Power of Self-Love

Once you have forgiven yourself and learned to unconditionally accept yourself, it is time to move on to *believing* in yourself. Whether you had parents like Helen Keller that believed in you, or even if this was not your parents' strong point, there *is* hope. *God* believes in you. *I* believe in you. And as YOU begin to believe in you, you will begin to realize that you *can* succeed in whatever you set your mind to.

HER STORY

There once was a young black girl. She enjoyed school not only because she enjoyed learning, but because it helped her forget the harsh reality of her life. She was a beautiful, smart little girl. Unfortunately, however, this young third-grade student seemed to many to be destined to failure. The color of her skin was just the beginning. On top of that, she came from a poor family. While she loved her parents, they had not been her best role-models. In short, most people at the time would probably have agreed that the chances of her life amounting to anything significant were slim.

But one day the little girl wrote a report for her third grade teacher. Unlike most children her age she handed in her finely-written report well in advance of the due date. The teacher, impressed with her timeliness and her talent for writing, wisely gave her the praise she deserved and even made a point of telling other teachers how proud she was of this particular student.

This now famous woman still remembers that experience. In fact, by her own account, it formed a solid foundation which helped her love and believe in herself and her ability to be successful. Years later, by all accounts, Oprah Winfrey is a happy and indisputably successful woman that millions, including myself, admire and look up to.

QUESTION

Had Oprah been raised to love and believe in herself? Did her parents teach her about the importance of unconditional self-acceptance? Did she begin to trust in her abilities just because? I would venture a guess that the answer to these questions is "no." However, through one small but significant experience, she began to understand her potential for greatness. This understanding helped her overcome many obstacles on the road to success.

Just like Oprah, you too can begin to love and believe in *yourself*, regardless of the way you were raised. You, too, are a wonderful person, capable of doing anything you put your mind to! The first step is to examine where you are right now when it comes to the question of self-love. Take the following self-quiz to find out.

Check off each item that applies to you in the "My Life WITHOUT Self-Love" column. Then, go to "My Life WITH Self-Love" and see what incredible, positive changes you can experience when you allow self-love to become a part of your life.

My Life WITHOUT Self-Love	My Life WITH Self-Love
__ I often criticize myself when I make a mistake	__ I recognize that mistakes are a part of life and try and learn from them
__ I lack confidence in my own abilities	__ I believe in myself and have confidence in my abilities
__ I can become easily irritated by the actions of others	__ What others do doesn't really bother me
__ I have difficulty finding reasons to be happy about my life	__ I can list all kinds of reasons to be happy about my life
__ I look forward to becoming old and dying	__ I hope to live a long, healthy life
__ I believe in the phrase "Life's tough and then you die"	__ Life has it's challenges, but I can handle it
__ I lack confidence in my ability to remember things	__ My memory is constantly improving
__ I seem to fail at everything I do	__ I try my best in everything I do
__ I often feel discouraged and hopeless when I think about my life	__ I am excited when I think about my life and all the wonderful possibilities
__ I have thought about suicide	__ Even in discouraging circumstances, I can see joy and hope
__ I have difficulty forgiving and letting go of the past	__ I forgive myself and others and let go of guilt from past mistakes
__ I wish that I could live someone else's life	__ I love my life and recognize that it is a work in progress

Now that you have read through the comparison of self-love vs. no self-love, which side of the chart is more true for you? If most of the things that rang true for you were located in the "no self-love" category, that's OK. A lack of self-love is very common and is, as they say, "subject to change." The important thing is beginning to make the necessary life changes that will enable you to love yourself from now on.

SELF-LOVE DEFINED

One of the dictionary definitions of "self-love" is: *Desire of personal happiness; tendency to seek one's own benefit or advantage.*

Q: How will you know when you are moving in the right direction?

A: You will be concerned for your personal happiness and well-being, and take actions to ensure it, just as you would if you were the loving parent of *yourself*.

So what exactly does a life with self-love look like? The following are some practical examples:

EXAMPLE 1

During a long day of work and taking care of your children, you promise yourself you will reward yourself with a hot bath once the dishes are done and everyone is asleep. At the end of the day when the dishes really are done, and your children really are sleeping, you ignore piles of laundry, floors that need scrubbing, and even the ringing phone, and *keep* your promise to yourself.

EXAMPLE 2

When you make a silly mistake at work, you stop and think before you speak your usual self-degrading words to yourself or your co-workers: "Boy, am I ever an idiot! Why can't I ever get this right?!"

Instead, you decide to acknowledge your mistake while still treating yourself kindly. You say to yourself or your co-workers something like: "Oops, I wish I wouldn't have done that! This is really unfortunate. Oh well, I guess I can chalk this up as a good learning experience and remember to do it right from now on."

EXAMPLE 3

In an effort to "win" a heated argument, you bring up an issue from the past that you know will really hurt your spouse. Reflecting on it a few hours later, you realize that your strategy worked very well.

But instead of being happy with your "victory," you begin to put yourself in the position of your partner. You recognize that what you said was very hurtful and wrong. After letting go of your anger and resentment, you sincerely apologize and reassure your sweetie pie that you still love and care for them.

• • •

When you love yourself, changes like the ones I have just mentioned will become a natural part of who you are. These deep changes will positively influence the way you speak, act and think. By *continuing* to love yourself and by building a solid relationship with *yourself*, you will become empowered to create and sustain a state of Mental Wellness throughout your life.

CHAPTER 2

Filling Your Own Bucket

BUCKET ANALOGY

Related to Secret 2, Putting on Your Oxygen Mask, is the "Filling Your Own Bucket" Theory, a concept I learned from my wife and a task which I consider a life-long goal. My explanation of this theory goes kinda like this:

Imagine that you are camping in a beautiful campground in the heart of the mountains. Your task is to go and pump water from the campground's only well – an old manual hand pump. After a few minutes of pumping water into your five gallon bucket you begin to get a little annoyed. For some unknown reason the bucket is as empty as when you started.

Surprised, you calmly put the bucket back under the spout and begin pumping again. This time you pump a little faster and a little harder, believing that maybe you just didn't try hard enough the first time. However, several minutes later, there are only a few drops of water at the bottom of the bucket!

Becoming a little frustrated, you slam the bucket down and try again, pumping as hard as you can, believing that you must be so dumb that you can't even fill a bucket with water. As you take a final look at the bottom of the bucket there is *still* no water! Annoyed, upset, and feeling like a failure for having not been able to complete such a simple task, you hang your head in shame and return to your campsite.

Believing that the problem must be technique, you share your sorrow with your wife and ask *her* to fill *your* bucket for you. After all, you think, she is much smarter and more capable than you are. "She will be able to get the water into the bucket," you tell yourself. However, after asking her to complete the task for you, she explains that doing so is simply not possible. Then she points out the source of the problem – a large hole in the bottom of the bucket.

Feeling like a fool and becoming discouraged about your failure to even notice the hole, you again ask your wife if she would just fill it for you. Surprisingly, however, she declines. Instead, she tells you that it is *impossible* for her to get any more water into the bucket than you did, until YOU repair the hole.

BUCKET THEORY

Aimee first introduced me to "Bucket Theory" just before I left on my manic trip from Canada to the United States. She introduced the theory in response to my repeated pleadings for her just to "love me," "be kind to me," and "just accept me" the way I was. But the reality was, because I had a huge hole in the bottom of my bucket, my ability to *perceive and feel the love* that Aimee was *already* showing me, was next to impossible. In a nutshell: If *you* don't love *yourself* you will be incapable of feeling and accepting the love of others. By learning to love yourself, you are, in effect, repairing the hole in your bucket – the void created by a lack of self-love. Once you learn how to love yourself, you will no longer feel as if you need *someone else* to fill your bucket for you. You will be very capable of filling it all on your own.

CHAPTER 3

Meet Your Inner Cheerleader

A s you begin to work on loving yourself you will discover that you have a power within yourself that formerly did not exist. Along with filling your own bucket, you will also be introduced to what I like to call your "Inner Cheerleader."

GOOD TO MEET YOU!

Your "Inner Cheerleader" has always been with you. Problem is, about the same time you decided to stop loving and believing in yourself, you also stuffed a sock in your Inner Cheerleader's mouth! While he or she has been trying to spit it out ever since, a lack of self-love has rendered the sock immovable. ☺

Now that you are learning to love yourself, however, the sock will come out, and the silenced inner voice will come to life again. This voice will be your strength in situations of all kinds. When you are facing a difficult life challenge, your Inner Cheerleader will shout: "You can do it! Don't give up!" When you have failed at something that was really important to you, your Inner Cheerleader will exclaim: "Hey, that's okay. Failure is a natural part of life. The important thing is that you tried your best." And, when you have achieved something really great in your life, your Inner Cheerleader will jump for joy and tell you "I knew you could do it! You worked hard and you deserve this success!"

MEET YOUR INNER CRITIC

If you find that your Inner Cheerleader does not immediately return, the problem may be that he or she is embarrassed to cheer for you in front of your "Inner Critic."

Your Inner Critic is the inner voice that replaced your Inner Cheerleader so many years ago. Having quite a different personality and attitude than your Inner Cheerleader, your Inner Critic reacts in an almost opposite way to every situation. Listening to the voice of your Inner Critic has contributed greatly to all the less-than-desirable situations in your life – including failing to sustain Long - Term Mental Wellness.

When you are facing a difficult life challenge, your Inner Critic will shout: "You *can't* do it! Give up, dummy!" When you have failed at something that was really important to you, your Inner Critic will exclaim: "Why did you even bother? If you had half a brain you'd realize there was no point even trying in the first place!" And, finally, when you have achieved something really great in your life, your Inner Critic will shake her head, roll her eyes and tell you "Wow, you did something right for *once*! It must have been luck, though, because you know in your heart that you are dumb and incapable. On top of that, you just don't deserve success!"

So how do you go about permanently silencing your Inner Critic and building a positive, long-term relationship with your Inner Cheerleader? Keep reading to find out!!

CHAPTER 4

Sticking Up for Yourself

MY STORY

B eing unaware of my Inner Critic and Inner Cheerleader for years, I was unaware of the struggle that was going inside myself. However, after being released from the hospital and becoming determined to do whatever if took to sustain Life – Long Mental Wellness, I quickly realized what was going on.

As I immersed myself in an intense study of "self-help" literature, I realized that I had ignored my Inner Cheerleader for a long time. Thankfully, however, as I began to love and believe in myself, I recognized the "voice" of my Inner Cheerleader. That "voice" motivated me to treat myself well and helped me see that I was a normal human being capable of taking care of myself and achieving success.

ADVICE FROM A BEST-SELLING AUTHOR & LIFE COACH

In her book, *Stand up for Your Life*, Cheryl Richardson discusses our abilities. She says: "You have deep within you the power to fulfill your highest vision of your life. To engage this power you MUST develop a solid, personal relationship with *yourself*. By doing so, you'll tap into a wealth of inner strength that will allow you to take the necessary actions that build confidence and self-esteem." Throughout her book, which I highly recommend, the importance of building a "rock-solid relationship" with yourself is mentioned again and again.

To be completely open, I must admit that after I read about the concept of developing a relationship with myself (of all people!), it struck me as being a little bit funny and weird. I thought to myself: "Of course I have a great relationship with myself. I've lived with myself for many years and have done many things with myself. In fact, I have literally spent *every* second, *every* minute, *every* hour, and *every* day for the last 30 years with *me!*" I rationalized that, because of this fact, I *must* have a good relationship with myself.

I continued along that line of thinking until I asked myself the question: "How true am I to myself?" My answer: If I was to look at myself from the outside - as if I were observing someone else - I was failing miserably. For example, when I would make a mistake, I would show little self-loyalty by criticizing myself or beating myself up. I would say something like: "Oh, Dave, you are so dumb, why did you do that?!" Because I was so hard on myself and engaged in *constant* self-criticism, I didn't ever accomplish much.

But everything changed when I learned about loving and accepting myself unconditionally, as well as the importance of building a rock-solid relationship with *me*. With this new understanding I realized that, despite my frequent self-criticism, *I really didn't even know* the person I was criticizing!

Now that I have worked hard to build a "rock solid relationship" with myself, all that has changed. Today I can proudly say that I have a great relationship with myself, and that it is getting even better on a daily basis. One of the best side-benefits of this relationship with myself is how it has affected my relationships with others. Establishing a better relationship with me has also led to better relationships with my wife, my children, and even my mother and father.

So, how do *you* go about building this "rock-solid relationship" with yourself? How do *you* stop treating yourself in a very harsh, rude way ? In *Stand Up For Your Life*, Cheryl Richardson describes the process. While I will leave it to you to buy her book and research most of the process for yourself, I want to discuss one aspect of building this relationship here and now. That is, the importance of setting boundaries.

CHAPTER 5

The Power of Setting Boundaries

S etting boundaries, according to Cheryl Richardson, is "the act of drawing imaginary lines around ourselves in order to protect us from the harmful behaviour of others." (I would also suggest that harmful behaviour can come from ourselves). When I learned about the concept and importance of setting boundaries, I immediately made a firm decision to begin setting boundaries in my own life. Looking back at the way my boundary-less life *used* to be, I can now see that setting and maintaining my boundaries has yielded amazing results.

MY STORY

The first person I set boundaries with was *me*. Yup, you read right – *me*. I told myself that regardless of how hard I had been on myself for so many years, my self-berating behaviour was no longer acceptable.

For example, instead of telling myself what an idiot I was for making a mistake, I stopped myself and examined what I was saying. Still acknowledging my mistake, I gave myself the benefit of the doubt and allowed myself to have another shot at getting it right. I also tried to remind myself of the inevitability of mistakes given the fact that I am an imperfect person. On top of that, I made a firm decision to be more kind to myself in every area of my life and treat *myself* with the amount of kindness and understanding I would have if I was dealing with our two-year-old daughter.

SETTING BOUNDARIES WITH AIMEE

After having successfully set boundaries with myself, I decided it was time to move to other key relationships. I began first with my wife, Aimee.

MY STORY

As we were driving to the store one day, Aimee criticized my decision to turn left to get to our destination. She insisted that turning right would have been a much smarter thing to do and that my decision would result in a lot of wasted time. Wanting to seize my opportunity to set boundaries, I remembered Cheryl Richardson's advice about being firm while maintaining an attitude of love and kindness. I said to Aimee something like: "Honey, do you *realize* that you just criticized me for simply making a left turn?"

After admitting that she was aware of what she had done, I explained that her criticism was no longer acceptable to me. I also explained that I was more than happy to have an honest, adult discussion about any potential concerns about my left turn, as long as she did not engage in put-downs. Finally, I explained that I would try my best to do the same for her.

Later, we discussed how well my boundary-setting had worked in improving my relationship with *myself* along with my belief that setting boundaries with her, and her with me, would probably help improve *our* relationship with *each other*.

From that moment on our relationship *did* begin to improve. Although things were a little rough in the beginning, as I continued to maintain my boundaries, Aimee began to respect what I was doing. And as she continued to maintain *her* boundaries, *I* began treating *her* with more respect too.

Over time the criticism and arguing slowly decreased almost to the point of non-existence. Since that time, the quality of our relationship has improved dramatically. In short, setting boundaries has helped us to fall in love all over again.

SETTING BOUNDARIES WITH MY MOTHER

Several weeks after setting my boundaries with Aimee, I realized that there was yet another important person in my life with whom I needed to set boundaries. And, while I was sure this would be even more challenging than setting boundaries with myself or Aimee, I knew it had to be done.

The day I received a scathing email from my mother, I recognized my opportunity to set my boundaries. With as much love and kindness as I could muster, I firmly let her know that her harsh treatment of me was no longer acceptable. While I knew that my words would not be well-received, I felt satisfied that I was doing the right thing and that eventually, setting boundaries with my mother would *improve* our relationship.

To make a long story short, although it took some time, setting boundaries with my mother proved to be a great benefit in my life and hers. In the same way that my relationship with myself and Aimee improved quickly and dramatically, my new relationship with my mother has never been better.

If you can relate to the examples I have described but have not yet set boundaries, consider the possibility that it is time to stop being pulled around by the whims of others. It is time to stop allowing others to criticize or show disrespect to your best friend – *you*. It is time to trust yourself and have confidence that you can decide for *yourself* what is best for *you*.

As you start by setting and maintaining boundaries with *yourself* you will find the inner strength you need to do the same with other important people in your life. Doing this will empower you to take the next step in achieving your goal of sustaining Life - Long Mental Wellness.

Step 2:
Learning to Use the Power of Promises

CHAPTER 6

Cultivating Self-Trust: The Key to Emotional Stability

IMAGINATION ACTIVITY

Imagine that your daughter's 8th birthday is coming up in 2 months. You know she has been anticipating this eventful day ever since her last birthday. Then, a few weeks before her big day, she asks you one simple question: "Mom/Dad – are you going to come to my birthday party or will you be working?" Of course, you assure her that you will make a point of attending the party despite your busy schedule.

However, the night before the party, you decide that you are just too busy to go. On top of being busy, thinking of all the annoying, noisy children that will be in your house begins to make you sick. As you think of the mess and the noise you think you feel a headache coming on.

The next day, as she is eating breakfast, you break the news to your daughter: You are too busy and have decided not to come. As expected, her feelings are deeply hurt and she begins to cry. When she reminds you that you *promised,* you tell her that it is just too difficult for you. The more she cries the more defensive and angry you become. Eventually, you walk out of the house, annoyed by *her* immaturity and lack of understanding.

MY EXPERIENCE

Sound a little unbelievable? I hope so! If you are anything like I was, however, you may often betray your *own* trust. Not following through with what you have promised *yourself* is just as serious as breaking a promise to a young child.

Whether we realize it or not, breaking promises to ourselves is very upsetting to the precious, trusting child that still exists in each of us. Even though you may have learned to tune out the cries of anger and self-betrayal, these feelings are real and are often manifested by moodiness and emotional instability.

EXPERT ADVICE

Stephan Covey, one my favourite self-help authors, describes a cure for promise-breaking in his best-selling book *The 7 Habits of Highly Effective People.* He states: "As we make and keep commitments, even small commitments, we begin to establish an inner integrity that gives us the awareness of self-control and the courage and strength to accept more of the responsibility for our own lives. By making and keeping promises to ourselves and others, little by little, our honor becomes greater than our moods."

If you find that you are betraying yourself by repeatedly making and then breaking promises to yourself, the time has come to STOP!

Examine your life. Think about what is *really* important to you. If you are betraying yourself, and if you continue on in the way you are going, you will have a really, really hard time respecting and *loving* yourself.

On the other hand, consistently making and keeping promises to yourself and others will go a long way in creating the emotional and mental stability you need as you work toward your goal of achieving sustained Mental Wellness.

THREE RULES OF THUMB

If the concept of making and keeping promises to yourself is new to you, here are some things to keep in mind:

1. Don't make a promise you don't intend to keep.

   • Doing this with yourself or others weakens trust. If you say you are going to do something – DO IT.

2. Think twice before making a promise.

   • When I was a young child, my Dad tried to get me to promise I would stop hitting my younger sister. Although I really wanted to please my father, I refused to *promise* that I would never hit her again. My reasoning, which he agreed with, was that if I forgot for a moment, and did hit her again, I would be *breaking* my promise. I had been taught by my father that a *promise was just as good as a "blood oath."*

3. Use promises sparingly

   • As Stephan Covey suggests, it is important to be careful to whom we make a promise, and about what we commit to do. Using promises *only in those situations that you are 100% committed to and absolutely sure you can deliver on*, will strengthen your level of trust in yourself, and increase your trustworthiness with others.

WHAT MAKING AND KEEPING PROMISES "LOOKS" LIKE

- If you promise yourself you will get up at 6am, you ensure that you go to bed the night before at a time that will facilitate you keeping your promise. In the morning you do it – no matter how tired you are – no questions asked.

- If you promise yourself you will take a relaxing weekend off work, you take the weekend off regardless of how difficult keeping your promise may be.

- If you promise yourself you will only have two chocolate chip cookies on a specific day, you put the bag back in the cupboard – *even if the cookies are calling your name*!

- If you promise your husband, your wife, your son, your daughter, or anyone, that you will do something, you *ensure that you do it!*

THE BOTTOM LINE

As you continue to consistently make and keep promises – even when it's tough – you will continue to build and strengthen trust. As this process continues, the quality of the relationship you have with yourself and with others will continue to improve, and you will develop a deep respect and love for yourself.

CHAPTER 7

The Big Benefits of Self-Trust

Interestingly, many people who struggle with a Mental Illness seem to gravitate to people whose opinions they believe in more than their own: psychologists, psychiatrists, social workers, good friends and family members.

MY STORY

If you have "been there," I'm sure you can relate to the multitude of challenges associated with hospitalization. For me, one of the biggest things I had to deal with - besides trying to get well enough to leave - was what to do about my constant confusion in making important decisions relating to *my* Mental Health. I felt as if I was being pulled from so many different directions I just didn't know *what* to do or *whom* to listen to!

My psychiatrist, whom I trusted, informed me that becoming well would only happen by taking psychiatric drugs. My parents, on the other hand, were completely *against* me taking psychiatric drugs. They tried their best to convince me that taking natural supplements was the only way I would become Mentally Well.

On yet another hand, Aimee had a different opinion. While she was willing to consider using natural supplements *later*, she agreed with my psychiatrist that drug therapy *now* would be the quickest way to get me Mentally Well and out of the hospital.

And then there was *me*, the person everyone had forgotten about! Little old *"me"* was *so* confused that in some ways I was happy to have the protection of a mental institution to figure it all out! However, as far as being in a situation that was "driving me crazy," I didn't have to worry – I was already there!

Bottom Line: I really didn't know *whose* opinion to trust. The only thing I was really convinced of, was that *my* opinion was not valid. And I did not trust *myself* to make the right decision.

Having three credible options, I decided to go with my wife, Aimee. I reasoned that she was the one with the most at stake. She was ultimately the one who would have to live with the long term consequences of whatever decision was made.

If I had it to do over again, trusting Aimee is a decision I wouldn't change. What I would have changed, however, is the level of trust I had in myself. In fact, I am *now* convinced that if I had developed trust and confidence in myself long before going to the hospital, I probably wouldn't have ended up there at all.

PART 9

TAKING CARE OF YOUR MENTAL & PHYSICAL NEEDS

Becoming your own best friend and keeping promises to yourself begins the journey to satisfying your emotional needs. With these emotional needs satisfied, we are ready to move into the final phase of the journey towards Life – Long Mental Wellness.

The 3rd Step in this Three-Step Program involves working on the fulfillment of your basic physical needs. Making and keeping promises forms the foundation for success in this phase.

STEP 3
BUILDING A SOLID FOUNDATION FOR WELLNESS: TAKING
CARE OF YOUR BASIC NEEDS

CHAPTER 1

Respecting Your Body's Need for Sleep

MY STORY

Growing up I learned "legends" of the methods soldiers would use in an attempt to break the will of their Prisoners of War. Confinement in small spaces, dripping water on the forehead or even putting slivers under the fingernails proved very helpful in getting a prisoner to "talk."

The war in Iraq has proven that there is also another less morbid but very "beneficial" tactic in eliciting crucial information from the enemy. That tactic is simple sleep deprivation. Why? Even the most strong-minded person can *eventually* become mentally weak if deprived of sleep.

When it comes to sleep, experts tell us that sleep is just as important as food and water for survival. They also agree that a lack of sleep can lead to a number of problems ranging from lack of energy and irritability to difficulty remembering things and feeling depressed.

As you discovered earlier in *The Mentally Ill Mentor*, several years ago I wound up in a very "high," manic state of mind. A *major* contributing factor behind my manic state was sleep deprivation.

In my sleep deprived state I had a *very* difficult time concentrating on solving any of the enormous marriage and family problems I *thought* I had. In my "weakened mental state," I was convinced that my wife hated me. I was sure that divorce was the only answer to our seemingly huge marriage problems. At the same time, I became convinced that everyone at work hated me and was out to get me. As my sleep deprivation continued, this false perception became my reality.

Having analyzed the reasons behind my sleep deprivation, I have come to the conclusion that *I* was the cause. My mind and body cried out for sleep but I paid little attention. Finally coming to a point of total exhaustion, I remember feeling extremely scared. While I was sane enough to know that I was *completely* out of control, I was so close to *insane* that I felt helpless to do anything about it!

Then, when I was hospitalized, I was injected with strong medication. In part, this was to help me get the sleep I desperately needed, which my doctors knew would aid in my return to a normal frame of mind.

WHY SLEEP?

Just like eating food and drinking water is absolutely critical in sustaining life, getting enough sleep is *absolutely critical* in creating and maintaining Mental Wellness. Just like many other things in life, the phrase "not too little, not too much" is a good rule of thumb when it comes to sleep.

No matter where you are on the "sleep spectrum," the great thing is that as you perfect the art of loving and taking care of *yourself*, your ability and *desire* to satisfy this most basic need will increase.

HOW MUCH SLEEP DO YOU NEED?

Sleep experts tell us that approximately 8 hours is the optimum amount of sleep. Opinions are varied on issues such as people who are "night owls" and people who can "survive" or even "thrive" on much less sleep. In any case, about 8 hours seems to be the general, ballpark target. Almost all sleep experts agree that you will know if you have had enough sleep if you can wake up in the morning without the aid of an alarm clock (or children)!

BENEFITS OF THE RIGHT AMOUNT OF SLEEP

You may not remember the last time you felt really rested. However, you *can* make changes. Now that you are working on loving yourself you will be able to cultivate the desire and self-discipline you need to make important changes in your sleep patterns.

Doing so will help you in many ways:

- More energy
- A greater feeling of overall happiness
- Greater emotional stability
- Increased ability to have a positive attitude
- Better memory
- Increased ability to focus
- Better overall health

If the amount of sleep you get each night is not what it should be, don't be too hard on yourself. Just make a decision that *from now on*, you will begin to take care of this basic need. To do this, simply identify your barriers to sleep.

These barriers may include:

- Shift Work

- Young Children

- Outside noise from traffic, trains, neighbours, or whatever

- Restlessness

- Inside Noise (snoring of partner or self)

- Uncomfortable bed

- Worry

- Stress

Now that you have identified the barriers you can work on removing them. Listed below are some helpful suggestions:

- **Shift Work**: Get a new job

- **Young Children**: If your spouse or significant other lives with you, trade off if possible. If not, take catnaps during the day whenever you can.

- **Outside Noise**: Use earplugs or move to a quieter location.

- **Restlessness:** Exercise. Exercising helps you feel more energetic when you are awake. It will also help you get into a deeper sleep each night.

- **Inside Noise (snoring):** Use earplugs, move rooms, and/or research the latest methods to prevent snoring.

- **Uncomfortable Bed:** Since we spend *one-third* of our lives asleep on our beds, it is worth every penny to invest in a new one.
- **Worry:** Read Dale Carnegie's *How to Stop Worrying and Start Living*.
- **Stress:** Write in your journal regularly. This will help mentally relieve the pressure and stresses of the day.

For most of us, getting the right amount of sleep is an ongoing challenge. If this is true for you, try viewing sleep as a simple, practical way to improve the state of your Mental Health.

As your efforts to get adequate sleep improve, you will begin to experience incredible benefits. You will feel an increased level of self-confidence and happiness and you will ultimately have a much greater ability to create for yourself the successful life you have always wanted.

BONUS SLEEP SOLUTION

Several years previous to going through my challenges with Mental Illness, I heard about this thing called meditation. While there are many good books on the subject written by experts, the meditation technique *I* use most often is what I refer to as "Simple Meditation." For me, this easy-to-implement technique works *very* well when it comes to relaxing and/or going to sleep.

A HOW-TO GUIDE TO "SIMPLE" MEDITATION

Taught to me by a very wise, calm, and relaxed man, this method involves simple visualization and proper breathing. It can be used anytime of the day or night whenever you need to relax or fall asleep.

Here's what you do:

- Breathe in through your nose and picture your breath going down your throat and swirling around in your lungs. When you have taken in all the air you can comfortably handle, envision your breath swirling the opposite way, leaving your lungs, going up your throat, and finally, out your nose again.

Although this technique is simple, I can tell you from experience that it really works! As you take deep breaths your brain will get the oxygen it needs and your heart rate will decrease. On top of those benefits, by focusing *only* on your breath, your mind will be freed from its intense focus on your worries, stress, or other barriers to sleep.

Now that you are serious about creating and maintaining Life - Long Mental Wellness and Success, *it is time to get serious about sleep.* Combined with your ever-increasing ability to show love to yourself and take care of yourself, getting the right amount of sleep will go a long way in helping you achieve and maintain the state of Mental Health you have always wanted.

CHAPTER 2

Respecting Your Body's Need for Food and Water

LESSONS FROM THE TSUNAMI

Only a short time ago very few of us would have imagined that an earthquake underneath the Indian Ocean could have caused a giant tsunami to form, killing hundreds of thousands of people.

As I'm sure you recall, after the tsunami struck, the world quickly mobilized to send aid to the survivors. Through governments and corporations, as well as private donations, *billions* of dollars were raised within a matter of weeks – a wonderful testament to the willingness we each have to help each other in a real-for-real crisis situation. The money collected, it was said at the time, would go toward providing the basic necessities of life – including food, clean water, and shelter.

If you are one of the millions of people throughout the world who donated money or volunteered in some way to help victims of this tragic world event, give yourself a pat on the back – you deserve it.

But when it comes to providing for *your* basic needs on a daily basis, how are *you* doing? Even though you probably have plenty of food in the refrigerator, do you ever deprive yourself by skipping breakfast, lunch or dinner? When you do eat regular meals do you ensure they meet your body's needs for nutrition?

What about clean water? Do you drink the water your body needs on a daily basis or do you substitute sugar-filled drinks such as soda, juice, coffee or tea to satisfy your thirst?

THE ROLE OF SELF-LOVE IN GOOD EATING HABITS

As you may have already guessed, poor eating habits stem from a lack of self love. Period. And, as I'm sure you have also guessed, now that you are deeply committed to maintaining long-term Mental Wellness, correcting your poor eating habits is top priority.

MY STORY

Looking back, as I progressed from my initial state of Mental Wellness into "hypo-mania" (near mania), and then "full-blown mania," my eating habits became worse and worse. I went from skipping breakfast to skipping breakfast and lunch, to barely eating anything in an entire day! When I did eat, I felt like taking the time to do it was an enormous burden. As a result, I would eat whatever was fast and easy to put in my mouth. Often, this included a lot of "garbage."

All that changed, of course, upon entering the hospital. There, regular, nutritious meals became the order of the day. With three "square" (nutritious and filling) meals a day, along with medication and sleep, it wasn't long before my Mental State returned to normal.

STARVING YOURSELF

For reasons unknown to me, many in our society put work, school, sports, making money, and everything else under the sun *ahead* of taking time to eat regular meals and drink lots of water. I guess they consistently neglect their human need for food and water in favour of doing other things they *think* are more important. Yet, as we all agreed in the middle of the Tsunami Crisis, food and clean water are absolutely essential to sustaining physical and mental health.

WHAT YOU CAN DO

As you improve in your ability to treat yourself in loving ways, it will become increasingly easier to put a high priority on ensuring you get the food and water you need. If it helps, think of a young child you love, and ask yourself if you would deprive him or her of food in the same way you deprive *yourself*.

If you haven't been eating properly up to now, that's okay. Forget the past and make a firm decision to change. You see, when you really think about it, depriving yourself of food and water when there is plenty to go around is crazy! To achieve your goal of creating and maintaining Life - Long Mental Wellness and Success, it is time to get serious about eating regular, nutritious meals and drinking plenty of water.

Observing these three simple "Eating Rules" will help:

EATING RULES

1. Make a decision to stop skipping meals and stick to it.

    *   Realize that *nothing* is more important in sustaining your life

than eating food and drinking water. You can also remind yourself that skipping meals can make your blood sugar drop to very
low levels, which can make you feel mean and grouchy.

2. Take time to eat

• Now that you are committed to eating at least three meals a day,
slow down!! Even though it may be tough, put the highest priority on carefully putting into your body that which you would
die without! Consider your slow, non-rushed meals an act of
self-love.

3. Eat *good* food and drink *lots* of water

• Now that you are committed to three non-rushed meals a day,
try your best to make them nutritious. If doing this is difficult,
think of your body as an expensive vehicle that works best with
high quality fuel. In addition, ensure that you drink lots of water. Among numerous other benefits, water enables your body
to properly carry out its normal functions. Lastly, even if you are
eating right, adding a nutritional supplement like a multi-vitamin can be very beneficial.

Don't wait for a natural disaster or a trip to your local Mental
Institution before you place a high priority on fulfilling your basic needs.
By consistently following these three simple Eating Rules you will dis-
cover for yourself the great benefits I am talking about.

CHAPTER 3

Exercise: The Secret to Dealing with Stress

U nless you have just come from another planet, it probably isn't really big news that exercise is good for you. In our modern age of health consciousness we are constantly told about the benefits of exercise in maintaining our physical health. That said, you may still be unaware of the incredible and positive *mental* benefits of exercise.

MY STORY

As the father of four adorable, healthy, energetic young children I feel very blessed. Truly, they are a source of happiness and inspiration. However, the reality is, that raising children is not always easy. From keeping the peace to simply working to provide for their basic needs, children come as part of a "package deal," and that package *often* includes stress.

Before I learned to love and take care of myself, I found that my thoughts were frequently along these lines: "What are we going to do!? We barely have enough money to pay the rent and buy food for the month!" or "I wish I had more patience with my children! I feel so angry at them all the time! Why can't I be more kind to them?!"

While consistent exercise doesn't change *what* causes the stress in my life, it completely changes how I *perceive* that stress. When I exercise, my thoughts become more along the lines of : "It may be a tight month budget-wise, but we'll be just fine," and "I am so glad I have more patience with our children. They sure are a lot of work, but they are worth every second of it."

If you are not sold on regular physical exercise as a means of maintaining Life - Long Mental Wellness, ask yourself the following questions:

Q: "Who do I know that consistently exercises, and has done for years?"

Now, think of the first person that came to your mind and evaluate them:

Q: Do they seem to be emotionally or mentally unstable?

Q: Do they lack self-confidence?

Q: Are they frequently irritable?

Q: Are they often discouraged or depressed?

My guess is that you answered "no" to every single question. Why? Exercise also has incredibly positive *mental* effects. In short, most people who exercise regularly just don't suffer from these problems.

GETTING MOTIVATED

If you are anything like me, you may have had trouble beginning and then sticking to an exercise program. If you have, take comfort in the fact that you are not alone! Every gym in your city knows that, statistically speaking, only about 1 in 5 people who set a firm goal to consistently exercise will ever follow through with it!

So how can *you* get motivated to begin exercising consistently? Understanding exactly *what* exercise will do for your brain can help.

YOUR HAPPY PILL

Exercising is kinda like popping a "happy pill." When you take your "pill" you will feel less stressed, much happier, and more capable of having a positive outlook on life. One of the reasons for this is the fact that, when we engage in exercise, our brain chemistry begins to change. This fact applies to all people.

When we exercise, hormones called Endorphins are secreted and Serotonin levels (another brain chemical) increase. Research shows that these two factors decrease feelings of stress and increase our ability to be happy.

EXERCISE & SELF-ESTEEM

Again, thinking back to someone you know who consistently exercises, my guess is that they do not appear to suffer from self-esteem problems. The great thing is, with consistent exercise, you can feel the very same way. After all, how can you *not* feel good about yourself when you consistently run 30 minutes a day, lift weights at the gym or whatever you may do to keep fit.

Bottom line: Self esteem is our body and mind's way of saying "thank you" for taking care of them.

MY STORY: FROM EXERCISE FAILURE TO CONSISTENT SUCCESS

A few years ago, after setting a goal to maintain my Mental Wellness for the long term, I decided that it was time to figure out how to motivate myself to exercise more consistently. Problem was, while I wanted the manly, muscle-building benefits from sit-ups, push-ups and weight training, engaging in these activities made me feel like I was in the army being trained for combat or even being punished. I decided that if I was going to succeed at consistently exercising it was time to find something I enjoyed.

Wanting to take care of my cardiovascular health *and* physical strength, I found an old rowing machine at a garage sale. After taking it home and learning how to properly use it, I fell in love with it and discovered that I really, really enjoyed how I felt after only a few minutes of rowing.

On top of that, as I listened to pump-up-type-music on my portable CD player, I forgot about the hard physical effort I was engaged in. Instead of being focussed on how much longer my demanding workout would take, I found myself fantasizing about the successful life I have always wanted to create for myself.

During the summer I also discovered that I love to run. Now I make sure I run or row at least five days a week for a minimum of 20 minutes each time. By mentally "escaping" for just 20 minutes a day, I no longer feel the need to escape the stress in my life by going manic. On top of that, I just don't feel as stressed as I used to. And when I encounter a potentially stressful situation, I have the ability to *deal* with the stress in a healthy, productive way.

BENEFITS OF EXERCISE

While the benefits of exercise may seem obvious, keeping them at the top of your mind can help you create desire and motivation.

Listed below are just a few of the many benefits of keeping yourself in shape:

- Weight loss

- Increased self-esteem

- Longer life

- More ability to handle life's inevitable stresses

- More happiness

- More positive outlook on life

- Better looking body

- Good example to children

- Regular time to yourself – like putting on your oxygen mask first

- Increased ability to love yourself, unconditionally accept yourself, and trust yourself

TIPS FOR CONSISTENT EXERCISE

In summary, everyone's body *and* mind has a need for exercise. If you are not yet at your desired level of Mental Wellness, consistent exercise is key in achieving your goal.

In list form, here is a summary of helpful exercise tips:

- Do something you love. Dr. Phil apparently plays tennis for 2 hours a day!

- Listen to pump-up-type music you love. Not only will this help you during exercise, but it will link happy feelings to your habit of daily exercise.

- While you exercise, get lost in another world. Fantasize about achieving your goals and fulfilling your hopes and dreams.

- Notice how you feel during and after you exercise. Write down your feelings in your journal and then re-read what you wrote when you are feeling unmotivated.

- Be realistic about your exercise. It's great to have the desire to run 2 hours a day, but if you don't have the time or inclination, setting this goal will only be setting yourself up for failure. Start small and keep your exercise to a level you can maintain for the long haul.

When I go running each morning I always find myself thinking this thought: If I can continue to do this, I can do anything! Truly, exercise is a catalyst which will help you to enjoy more fully, all that is good in life. Begin by enjoying long-term Mental Wellness and you will be well on your way to success in *every* area of your life!!

CHAPTER 4

Your Relationship with Sugar

As you begin getting the right amount of sleep, eating regular meals, drinking lots of water and exercising on a regular basis, it is time to consider one more aspect vital to your physical and Mental Health. That aspect involves your relationship with sugar.

MY STORY

For the first seven years of my married life, I continued to make the same mistake every year. During the Christmas holidays I would jack myself up with whatever sugar-laden treats I could find. As a result, I would enjoy a "sugar high" for several days. While it felt great to eat so much sugar, the inevitable crash from my sugar high was not quite as fun.

Year after year, as we would drive home from visiting with relatives having eaten tons of chocolate and other sugary junk food, I would feel a level of irritability and irritation that seemed uncontrollable. I perceived nearly every word that escaped Aimee's mouth as vicious and attacking. In response, I often attacked back, shocking myself and leaving my wife in tears.

Ashamed, but not understanding the main cause, this behaviour continued year after year, until one year it dawned on me! My sugar intake was a HUGE part of the problem. With that in mind, I decided to strictly limit how much sugar I ate during the holidays and keep it within the range I observed throughout the rest of the year.

PROBLEM SOLVED

Lowering my sugar intake made *all* the difference. On the next drive home following our annual Christmas visit with relatives, I was my usual self. No more irritability, no more false perceptions that Aimee was attacking me and no more nasty words in defence. Finally, I thought, I had discovered the secret to fixing my post-holiday emotional problems.

However, my incredible discovery still did not explain why Aimee, who ingested approximately the same amount of sugar in the same time frame, did not react in the same two-year-old-temper-tantrum way I did. The more I researched this and other topics, I came to the conclusion that I am just one of those people who is "sugar sensitive."

WHAT THE EXPERTS SAY

In her book *The Sugar Addicts Total Recovery Program*, best-selling author, Dr. Kathleen DesMaisons, explains: "If you are sugar sensitive and your meals are erratic, if you skip breakfast, eat lots of sweet things, eat quarts of diet soda or eat pounds of pasta and bread, then you will be depressed, moody, erratic, volatile, forgetful and impulsive." As someone who lived through all of those symptoms, I can attest to the truth of what Dr. DesMaisons writes.

In my experience, and from my research on the subject, it seems obvious that Mental Illness and sugar sensitivity often go together. However, whether you *think* you are sugar sensitive or not, decreasing your level of sugar intake and beginning to eat a more healthy, balanced diet will go a long way in reaching your goal of achieving and maintaining Life - Long Mental Wellness & Success.

While many books have been written about sugar sensitivity and the negative effects of a high sugar intake, at this point, I would like to suggest a few simple techniques for lowering the amount of sugar in your diet.

While the following suggestions may not sound easy, just remember: The higher the level of difficulty in implementing them, the greater the probability that you *really* need to!

As I have mentioned already, if you now recognize that you have a problem in this area, don't be too hard on yourself. Our North American society seems to thrive on marketing sugar, sugar, and more sugar. The important thing is that you *recognize* the existence of a problem and take immediate action to deal with it.

HELPFUL TIPS TO IMPROVE YOUR RELATIONSHIP WITH SUGAR

1. Do a quick and easy self-analysis. For one week, record everything you eat that you consider "junk" due to its high levels of refined sugar.

2. Once you have determined the level of your weekly sugar intake, set a realistic goal to lower it. While you may prefer to go "cold turkey," it may be easier to cut back little by little.

3. To cut back on your sugar intake, start by eliminating just one major source of sugar, such as a chocolate bar, every second day. As you do this, continue to *analyze* the other sources of sugar in your diet.

4. As you become accustomed to living with less sugar, increase the

rate at which you lower your sugar intake. Continue doing this until eating sugary foods and snacks is the exception to the rule. However, *don't go so far as to get a "Sugar Divorce"*! Although *completely* severing your relationship with sugar may seem like a good idea right now, you will probably regret it later. Because doing so can often lead to frustration, binging, and a promise to never go off sugar again, allow yourself to have a little sugar once in a while.

By cutting down on your sugar intake you may feel as if you are depriving yourself of one of the great things in life. If you do have these feelings just keep in mind that achieving and sustaining Life - Long Mental Wellness comes with a price, and it will be well worth the sacrifice!

PART 10
LIFE – LONG MENTAL WELLNESS
& SUCCESS

CHAPTER 1

Bringing It All Together

By respecting your body's needs and treating yourself in a loving, caring way, you will begin to experience a wonderful, perpetual cycle. As you treat yourself well, your level of self-love will increase. As your level of self-love increases, you will treat yourself even better. As you continue to experience the positive effects of this enjoyable, healthy, cycle, you will continue to experience success in *all* areas of your life.

As we near the conclusion of *The Mentally Ill Mentor*, let's review what we have learned in the last several chapters:

1. **Respecting Your Body's Need for Sleep**: Don't engage in sleep deprivation. This information-eliciting tactic effective for Prisoners of War is not in harmony with the concept of self-love. On the other end of the spectrum, ensure that you do not get *excessive* amounts of sleep either. Instead, decide to do *whatever it takes* to get the *right* amount of sleep. Whether you decide to find a new job, buy a new mattress, or pop in some earplugs at night, getting the proper amount of sleep is well worth the sacrifice.

2. **Respecting Your Body's Need for Food and Water**: The Tsunami crisis in Asia was tragic and heartbreaking. In your desire to help, you may have donated money to aid organizations, which

in turn provided food and clean water to survivors. But what about ensuring *you* get adequate food and water? If you haven't been, it is time to begin eating regular, nutritious meals and ensuring you drink plenty of water. I also recommend taking some type of "multi-vitamin" to make up for the nutrients some food may lack. Remember: Fulfilling your most basic human need for food and water is a manifestation of the love you have for yourself.

3. **Exercise: The Secret to Dealing with Stress:** Stress is simply a part of life. But *reacting* to stress in an unhealthy way no longer needs to be. By beginning an exercise program you enjoy, and by following it day after day, week after week, month after month, year after year, your ability to deal with stress in a healthy, productive way will skyrocket! You will also experience an increased level of self-esteem. On top of all that, you will become more balanced emotionally, and will have an even greater capacity to achieve and sustain Life - Long Mental Wellness and Success.

4. **Your Relationship with Sugar:** The good news is: Eating foods full of sugar *can* be a short term source of pleasure. The bad news: The long term negative effects far outweigh the short term benefits. If you are depressed, moody, and/or have a raging temper, consider the possibility that you are *sugar sensitive*. After "diagnosing" yourself, take *immediate* action by beginning to limit your overall sugar intake. While doing this may qualify as a major lifestyle change that will require self-discipline and sacrifice, the benefits to your emotional and Mental Health will be exquisite!

In reviewing these four points it is easy to see how implementing these suggestions will contribute significantly to achieving your goal of long-term Mental Wellness. In fact, at this moment, I hope that you are absolutely fired-up, excited, and ready to get going in making the changes that will improve your life, forever!

However, in a few short pages, you will reach the end of *The Mentally Ill Mentor*. And, while you can keep it by your bed as a frequent reference, in time, your excitement will inevitably die down. As it does, your memory of the important principles and techniques you have learned will begin to fade. So what can you do to ensure you keep these principles and practices at the top of your mind?

THE SOLUTION

They say a goal is only a dream until it is written down. To ensure your dream of long-term Mental Wellness becomes a reality, you have already signed a contract with yourself: *My Commitment To Life-Long Mental Wellness & Success*. To remind yourself of your commitment, put your contract on your bedroom wall, tape it to your bathroom mirror, or put it wherever you can to ensure you will see it often. In this way, you will continue to be reminded of your goal and commitment.

CHAPTER 2

The Power of Your Mental Wellness & Success Chart

MY STORY

After my hospitalizations, I felt a bit frustrated by how slowly I was progressing in returning to a state of Mental Wellness. Although I was committed to changing how I viewed myself and how I treated myself, I felt overwhelmed and sometimes confused by all the things I knew I needed to do.

Amid my frustration, my thoughts turned to the two-year mission I had served for my church. Willingly conforming to what some would call "strict" rules, all missionaries were asked to check off several categories on a chart at the end of every day. The chart was made up of various aspects of normal, disciplined mission life, such as personal scripture study and beginning the days' work at 9:30 a.m.

For me, this "Daily Self Examination" helped in the creation of some *very* positive habits which are still a major part of my life more than 10 years later.

THE MENTAL WELLNESS & SUCCESS CHART IS BORN

As I thought more about this system I reasoned that by adopting a similar system at home, I would be able to *accelerate* my rate of progress and more quickly accomplish my goal of achieving and maintaining long-term Mental Wellness.

To make a long story short, it worked! By putting a chart up on our bedroom wall, and by faithfully and honestly filling it out at the end of each day, I began to experience rapid progress. I am now convinced that the speed of this progress was a *direct* result of the charting system I adapted from my mission.

WHY KEEP TRACK?

Through using this charting system, I have experienced great benefits – benefits that you, too, can experience.

Using your Mental Wellness & Success Chart on a daily basis will enable you to:

1. Become responsible for *yourself* and your moods.

   • Instead of only depending on your spouse, your doctor, your parents or a trusted friend to assess the state of your Mental Health, you will become empowered to determine this for yourself.

2. Maintain a state of Mental Wellness

   • Not only will you be able to see for yourself when your Mental State is slipping, the likelihood of a Mental Illness getting out of control will be slim. This is simply because you will be able to nip small problems in the bud.

- Example: During your weekly review you notice that the rating assigned to your "mood" has been declining for several days. Realizing there is a problem, you check your "mood-affecting" categories. Your analysis shows that your sugar intake over the last week was *very* high. On top of that you check the "sleep" category and discover that you have gotten to bed late *every* night. To even out your moods, you decide to *limit* your sugar intake and *increase* your sleep. During your next weekly review your Self-Analysis shows that your moods are back to where they should be.

YOUR MENTAL WELLNESS & SUCCESS CHART

On the following two pages you will see two Mental Wellness & Success Charts. The first is a sample of the one I keep up on my bedroom wall. The second is a similar chart that you can copy and put up on your wall and personalize. Keep reading to find out what everything means and why tracking your progress is so important.

DAILY CANI CHART

Reward: $1.00 per day for 80% Success and above

Date	Arise 6 am	Exercise	Scrips	Prayer	MIM	Dish/BR	Bed 10:30	Sugar	Mood	
Total:										

Date	Arise 6 am	Exercise	Scrips	Prayer	MIM	Dish/BR	Bed 10:30	Sugar	Mood	
Total:										

Date	Arise 6 am	Exercise	Scrips	Prayer	MIM	Dish/BR	Bed 10:30	Sugar	Mood	
Total:										

Date	Arise 6 am	Exercise	Scrips	Prayer	MIM	Dish/BR	Bed 10:30	Sugar	Mood	
Total:										

MY MENTAL WELLNESS & SUCCESS CHART

Reward:

Date	Arise	Exercise	Breakfast	Lunch	Dinner	Water	Sugar	Mood	Bed	
Total:										

Date	Arise	Exercise	Breakfast	Lunch	Dinner	Water	Sugar	Mood	Bed	
Total:										

Date	Arise	Exercise	Breakfast	Lunch	Dinner	Water	Sugar	Mood	Bed	
Total:										

Date	Arise	Exercise	Breakfast	Lunch	Dinner	Water	Sugar	Mood	Bed	
Total:										

1. DAILY CANI CHART

You will notice that I have given my chart the title "Daily CANI Chart". CANI, an acronym created by one of my mentors and best-selling authors Tony Robbins, stands for: Constant And Never-ending Improvement. In his book *Awaken the Giant Within,* Tony discusses the importance of implementing the principle of CANI in all areas of our lives.

For me, and as it relates to my goal of maintaining Life - Long Mental Wellness & Success, CANI has to do with the things I do *each day* to continue to achieve my goal.

Feel free to title and adapt *your* chart in whatever ways you see fit.

2. REWARD: $1.00 PER DAY FOR 80% SUCCESS AND ABOVE

In *Awaken the Giant Within,* Tony also discusses the importance of linking pleasure to activities we would like to continue. Said another way, rewarding ourselves for a job well done helps create and maintain the desire to keep going.

When *I* achieve the level of success that I desire, I give myself a small, daily reward – usually one dollar. Then, every few weeks I take the money I have earned and buy a small gift for myself. I usually write down what I am going to buy on the top of my chart. This reminds me of my eventual reward and helps me to stay motivated. Then, if I find it hard to get up early, to go jogging in a snow storm, or to resist a donut that is calling my name, the thought of my reward helps me suck it up and do what needs to be done.

---

3. CATEGORIES – AN EXPLANATION OF MY CHART

As you can see, the rest of the chart is pretty self explanatory. When I get up at 6am, I put a check in that box. When I exercise, I put a check in that box, and so on.

- On my chart "Scrips" stands for Scripture Reading.

- "MIM" stands for "Mentally Ill Mentor". This is the category I use to track my progress in writing this book (a HUGE project!).

- "Dish/BR" is a category I added after a heart-to-heart conversation with Aimee. In an effort to improve on the amount of work I do around the house, I committed to doing dishes ("Dish") or cleaning the bathroom ("BR") on a daily basis.

- "Bed 10:30" helps remind me to get to adequate rest. If I do not get to bed at exactly 10:30 pm, I write in the actual time. Being aware of what time I go to bed each night allows me to quickly make a "course correction" if I end up getting to bed late several nights in a row.

- "Sugar": Being "sugar sensitive", I like to track how often I have foods or snacks with refined sugar in them – a piece of chocolate, a donut, or a drink of lemonade. While I believe in allowing myself to have *some* things that contain refined sugar, I try to limit my sugar intake by only having "junk" every second or third day. Since I have so little, when I do have sugar, I get a lot of pleasure from savouring a very small amount, as opposed to stuffing myself with tons of it.

- "Mood" is a category that helps me draw a correlation between how I feel and what I do on a daily basis. I assess my mood on a scale of 1-20. One (1) would indicate a very depressed state, while ten (10) indicates a mood that I consider ideal – not too high, not too low. On the high end of the scale, twenty (20) would indicate a state of mania. While my moods usually fall somewhere in the 9 or 10 range, I have discovered that fluctuations can occur. When they do, I can quickly track the cause: missing exercising, getting insufficient sleep, or having too much sugar.

- "Blank": I keep this category open for anything I may want to add in the future.

_____

YOUR DAILY CHART

Of course, I recommend personalizing your chart. In doing so, however, it is important to ensure you track the basics: Sleep, Regular Meals (Food & Water), Exercise, Sugar Intake and Mood.

If you want to add more categories like I have, feel free. However, I would suggest waiting at least 3-4 weeks in order to give yourself time to form a solid habit of taking care of the basics.

Perhaps the biggest benefit of using this tracking system is the positive effect it can have on *all* areas of your life. As you continue to cultivate self-love by taking care of your basic needs, you will *automatically* become empowered to take responsibility for your own Mental Health. By doing this, you will ensure a greater level of success in all areas of your life!

CHAPTER 3

You CAN Do It!!

If you are feeling a little overwhelmed with all the changes suggested in *The Mentally Ill Mentor*, don't be too concerned. It is perfectly normal to feel the way you do. Discouragement occasionally happens to nearly everyone.

MY STORY

When I feel overwhelmed, I make an effort to put my life into perspective. For me, reminding myself that the acronym CANI (Constant And Never-ending Improvement) is not IANI – *Instantaneous* And Never-ending Improvement is helpful. Change is often a slow and steady process.

While there are probably hundreds of things about yourself and your life that you would like to improve, remember that you have a lifetime to make the changes you want. For now, the important thing is just to focus on YOU, and your Commitment to Life - Long Mental Wellness & Success.

THE SPILL OVER EFFECT

As you put in an honest, sincere effort, you will *automatically* begin to experience positive changes in the state of your Mental Health. But wait, that's not all!

By *continuing* to focus on loving and taking care of *yourself,* all the other areas of your life will automatically improve too, a phenomenon I like to call The "Spill Over" Effect.

· · ·

YOUR STORY

With your *Commitment to Life-Long Mental Wellness & Success* signed and your *Mental Wellness & Success Chart* in place, you are ready to take *complete responsibility* for *your* life. Whether you do it literally or not, you are now ready to write YOUR Story.

As you use these tools, and as you continue to work on loving and taking care of yourself, you will experience significant, positive life changes. As you continue to internalize and live true to the principles and techniques outlined in this book, you will have the ability to achieve and maintain the long-term Mental Wellness you desire.

But if you are ever tempted to quit the fight or to give up on believing in *you,* just remember these three simple truths:

1. *Remember* that you are a Child of God who loves you. *Remember* that you can pray and ask for his help anytime, anywhere.

2. *Remember* that loving and believing in yourself will give you the power to accomplish anything you desire.

3. *Remember* to become a mentor – a wise and trusted counsellor or teacher – to others who need *your* help.

    Remember that if *I* can do it, so can *you*.

Your Mentally WELL Mentor,
David Grant Miller

www.TheMentallyIllMentor.com

For ongoing support during your journey to Mental Wellness, visit our website.

There you can access Dave's blog (online journal), uplifting and inspirational stories, sign up for a free newsletter and become connected with others who can relate to your struggles and successes.

BOOKS I LOVE & RECOMMEND

(in no particular order)

- 7 Habits of Highly Effective People by Stephen Covey
- Living the 7 Habits by Stephen Covey
- 7 Habits of Highly Effective Families by Stephen Covey
- The 8th Habit by Stephen Covey
- Journal of Mother Theresa
- Million Dollar Habits by Brian Tracy
- Mary Kay by Mary Kay Ash
- Practical Intuition in Love by Laura Day
- Unlimited Power by Anthony Robbins
- Standing for Something by Gordon B. Hinckley
- The Best of the Original Chicken Soup for the Soul by Jack Canfield and Mark Victor Hansen
- Chicken Soup for the Couples Soul by Jack Canfield and Mark Victor Hansen
- Chicken Soup for the Writer's Soul by Jack Canfield and Mark Victor Hansen
- The Man Who Listens to Horses by Monty Roberts
- Don't Worry, Make Money by Richard Carlson
- Don't Sweat the Small Stuff by Richard Carlson
- Don't Sweat the Small Stuff in Love by Richard and Kristine Carlson
- What About the Big Stuff? by Richard Carlson
- Men Are From Mars, Women Are From Venus by John Gray
- Children Are From Heaven by John Gray
- Practical Miracles for Mars & Venus by John Gray
- Mars & Venus in Love by John Gray

- Creating Health by Deepak Chopra
- On Forgiving Your Parents by Marianne Williamson
- Golf is a Game of Confidence by Bob Rotella and Bob Cullen
- Secrets for Success & Happiness by Og Mandino
- Iacocca – an Autobiography by Lee Iacocca (former head of Chrysler Corporation)
- How to Speak/How to Listen by Mortimer J. Adler
- Ask Barbara (100 Most Asked Questions About Love, Sex & Relationships) by Barbara deAngelis
- Stand Up For Your Life by Cheryl Richardson
- Love, Medicine & Miracles by Bernie Siegel
- Miracle Cures by Jean Carper
- Angel Encounters (True Stories of Divine Intervention) by Karen Goldman
- Your Erroneous Zones by Wayne Dyer
- How to Handle Conflict and Manage Anger by Denis Waitley
- What Matters Most by Hyrum Smith
- Awaken the Giant Within by Anthony Robbins
- Notes from a Friend by Anthony Robbins
- How to Never Grow Old by Bernie Siegel
- Boundless Energy by Deepak Chopra
- Thinking Skills for the 21st Century by Michael McCarthy
- The Power of Positive Thinking by Norman Vincent Peale
- Discover Your Genius by Michael J. Gelb
- Time Shifting by Stephen Rechtschaffen
- You Can Heal Your Life by Louise Hay
- As You Think (As a Man Thinketh) by James Allen
- Let Not Your Heart Be Troubled by Boyd K. Packer
- How to Win Friends and Influence People by Dale Carnegie
- How to Stop Worrying and Start Living by Dale Carnegie

- Training a Tiger by Earl Woods
- The Power of Focus by Jack Canfield, Mark Victor Hansen and Les Hewitt
- Powerful Prayers by Larry King
- Future Talk by Larry King
- Joseph Smith the Prophet by Truman G. Madsen
- Long Walk to Freedom by Nelson Mandela
- The Wealthy Barber by David Chilton
- How To Talk So Kids Will Listen & Listen So Kids Will Talk by Adele Faber and Elaine Mazlish
- Love and Survival by Dean Ornish
- The Dance of Anger by Harriet Lerner
- What Wives Expect of Husbands by Brent A. Barlow
- What Husbands Expect of Wives by Brent A. Barlow
- The Bible
- The Book of Mormon
- From Panic to Power by Lucinda Bassett
- First Things First by Stephen Covey
- 3 Steps to a Strong Family by Linda and Richard Eyre
- Fire Your Shrink! by Michele Weiner – Davis
- Real Magic by Wayne Dyer
- What Do You REALLY Want For Your Children? by Wayne Dyer
- The Power of Positive Parenting by Glenn Latham
- Ageless Body Timeless Mind by Deepak Chopra
- Guerilla Marketing for Writers by Jay Conrad Levinson

PERMISSIONS

ISBN 1-41206051-6